AWARENESS PUT ME ON

LEADING BY CHOICE, THRIVING BY DESIGN

CHANTÉE L CHRISTIAN
CHARLOTTE R. JACOBS, MBA, PCC, CPC, ELI-MP
CHENISE UPSHUR   ALAWNA RENEE OZOKA
TIFFANY JOY MURCHISON   KAYLEIGH O'KEEFE
SAMANTHA J.A. ARMSTRONG   ANDREW BEAMON
ANGELA DIXON WILLIAMS   TRINI K. SHERMAN
NIKKI WALKER   NAYSHONDRA MERCER, CPC, ELI-MP
DAVID C. ATKINS   RAMALL JOHNSON   J. ARTEL SMITH
KATHERINE N. JOHNSON, ACC, CPC, ELI-MP
ALEX DAVIS, CPA, CFP®   DYANA LANGLEY-ROBINSON
JANAE D. JOHNSON   HADY MÉNDEZ
SYLVEA HOLLIS, PHD   B. MARIE ADAMS

Foreword by
RANDI B.

Awareness Put Me On © 2024 CC Media

All Rights Reserved. Apart from any fair dealing for the purposes of research or private study, or criticism or review, as permitted under the Copyright, Designs and Patents Act 1988, this publication may only be reproduced, stored or transmitted, in any form or by any means, with the prior permission in writing of the copyright owner, or in the case of the reprographic reproduction in accordance with the terms of licenses issued by the Copyright Licensing Agency. Enquiries concerning reproduction outside those terms should be sent to the publisher.

Print ISBN: 979-8-9883816-8-6

Ebook ISBN: 979-8-9883816-9-3

DEDICATION

Thank you for choosing to embark on this transformative journey with us. In a world filled with countless book options, you've chosen Awareness Put Me On, and for that, we are truly grateful.

This book is dedicated to anyone who has ever felt unseen, unheard, misunderstood, or unworthy. Our hope is that through our shared yet personal experiences, you will feel seen, heard, understood, and worthy.

Know that dreams do come true. Ours did and still are!

CONTENTS

Foreword   9
Introduction   13

Part I
PERSONAL DEVELOPMENT

1. Charlotte R. Jacobs, MBA, PCC, CPC, ELI-MP   21
   Getting Out Of My Own Way

   About the Author   29

2. Chantée L. Christian   31
   Cease-AND-Desist the Internal BS

   About the Author   41

3. Chenise Upshur   43
   Chasing Peace

   About the Author   51

4. Alawna Renee Ozoka   53
   Reunite With Your Power

   About the Author   63

5. Tiffany Joy Murchison   65
   Setting Boundaries and Minding Your Own Business

   About the Author   77

6. Kayleigh O'Keefe   79
   Excellence in Awareness

   About the Author   87

Part II
LEADERSHIP & PROFESSIONAL DEVELOPMENT

7. Samantha J. A. Armstrong   91
   Journey to Authenticity: Navigating the Rhythm of Inner Truth

   About the Author   101

8. Andrew Beamon   103
   Empowering Excellence: From Imposter Syndrome to Authentic Leadership

About the Author	113
9. Angela Dixon Williams	115
The Blueprint of Authentic Leadership	
About the Author	127

Part III
RESILIENCE & TRANSFORMATION

10. Trini K. Sherman	131
Wisdom Through the Pivots	
About the Author	141
11. Nikki Walker	143
Stronger Than Pride	
About the Author	151
12. Nayshondra Mercer, CPC, ELI-MP	153
I Am: Seeking Myself	
About the Author	165
13. David C. Atkins	167
Navigating the Crossroads of Life	
About the Author	177
14. Ramall Johnson	179
Unpacking the Lessons Found on the Other Side	
About the Author	189
15. J. Artel Smith	191
From Struggle to Strength	
About the Author	199

Part IV
IDENTITY

16. Katherine N. Johnson, ACC, CPC, ELI-MP	203
Beauty Unveiled	
About the Author	213
17. Alex Davis, CPA, CFP®	215
From Shadows to Light: The Journey of Healing Beyond the Facade	
About the Author	225
18. Dyana Langley-Robinson	227
All the Shades of Gray	
About the Author	237

Part V
MINDFULNESS & REFLECTION

19. Janae D. Johnson, M.A. — 241
    Power in the Pause
    About the Author — 253
20. Hady Méndez — 255
    That Time I Ugly Cried
    About the Author — 265
21. Sylvea Hollis, PhD — 267
    Lessons in Listening From My First Marathon
    About the Author — 275
22. B. Marie Adams — 277
    2:00 AM Wake Up Call
    About the Author — 287

Acknowledgments — 289
Footnotes — 291
About Soul Excellence Publishing — 293

FOREWORD

BY RANDI B.

Bamboozled!

Looking back, I was bamboozled by the adults in my life. And you probably were, too.

Now I am not suggesting that the deceit was purposeful or malicious. On the contrary, I believe that when we were younger, the "grown-ups" around us were playing the role of adults: assuredly sharing advice about what we should and should not be doing, confidently making decisions, and masterfully using adulting-terms like goals, savings, and accountability. I think most of those adults innocently thought that the only lies they were telling us were about Santa Claus, the Easter Bunny, and how far they had to walk in the snow to school (uphill both ways!).

But they were lying (yep, I said it; and I'm a Southern, Black woman who was punished as a child if it even looked like my mouth was about to form the word "lie"). I dare say many of the adults we were around during our youth being fake (and faking it) much of the time.

Not one "adult" told me that they had no idea what they were doing. Never did I guess that most of them were only slightly less clueless about navigating life than I was. Turns out, that until our last breath, we are always still trying to figure out life; learning that life is a series of lessons and that the smartest people in the world continue to seek teachers to guide them. In other words, class always remains in session and we are all on a path of continuous learning and improvement.

And now you have joined us here, with over twenty authors sharing some of the lessons we've learned along our individual journeys (even though we, too, remain in school). Your presence tells me that you have realized a few things.

One, that you, too, have been bamboozled.

Two, life is the biggest and longest-lasting university in the world.

Three, you want to be on life's Honor Roll.

And four, you understand that we can all better accomplish our goals, feel supported and gain clarity when we rely on and learn from each other.

Consider us all classmates.

Awareness Put Me On is a course on key life lessons such as resilience, navigating systems, and conquering Imposter Syndrome. It includes lessons that I've learned yet on which I continue to need regular refresher courses. For instance, I haven't conquered Imposter Syndrome, but I've learned how to be a more formidable opponent of it. For example, when Chantée Christian (our "dean" of-sorts) asked me to write the foreword for this book, my immediate reaction was to decline. Yes, I write, and I have published a couple of books, but I'm not a "writer." Rather, I am the daughter (proud daughter) of Sandra Bryant, who laughed at me when I said I wanted to major in journalism so that I could be a writer, travel the globe, and eventually share stories with the world.

"Girl, you sound as crazy as a cuckoo! How many Black journalists do you see

on TV (this was the late 80's)? You can major in English so you can teach English. The way I see it, the only choice you need to make is between teaching middle or high school."

Though she has since died, and while she was an incredible mother overall, those words and their impact still live in me. They still form a subconscious wall that I must consciously work to overcome. But I have overcome.

While I initially followed my mother's guidance and became a high school English teacher after completing my master's degree, I learned it wasn't enough. I matured and eventually allowed my voice to be louder than my mother's and pursued my dreams. I founded an award-winning, successful consulting firm over 20 years ago. I've published two books and been a featured author in an anthology of essays compiled by Deborah Santana. I created a popular blog, travel the world, and now appear regularly on multiple media platforms.

Reading *Awareness Put Me On* not only allowed me to reflect on what I have overcome, but also provided insight and lessons on the work that remains in front of me. It energized me to do more with my life; inspired me to do better with family, career, lifestyle and self; and provided insights on tools and practices to do so.

The lessons of *Awareness Put Me On* are invaluable. In "Navigating the Crossroads of Life," David C. Atkins describes how a message from his mother created an internal conflict that he worked to actively overcome as he has journeyed through life.

Janae D. Johnson's reflections on the "Power in the Pause" offer valuable thoughts on the strengths and insights that are available when we choose to be consciously still and quiet.

Trini K. Sherman's writings about the wisdom that can be gained from life's challenges, and the need to pivot out of them, is a master class on resiliency. And Hady Méndez's thoughts on conquering your career, instead of letting your work conquer you, is sure to lead to both increased satisfaction and success. These examples are just a sampling of the many lessons to be learned. And we all benefit from continuing education along our journeys.

Welcome. Class is in session.

In Solidarity,

Randi B.

Author, Speaker, Entrepreneur, Host & DEI Disruptor

INTRODUCTION
BY CHANTÉE L CHRISTIAN

Are you ready for a change or just flirting with the idea?
Are you interested in increasing your awareness?

If your answer is a resounding "**YES**," then *Awareness Put Me On* is the book for you!

∾

A COLLECTIVE EXPLORATION INTO THE POWER OF INCREASED AWARENESS

This transformative book is designed to empower people just like you to lead from within, unlock your true potential, and ignite meaningful change. This book will feel like an immersive experience of self-discovery and empowerment, equipping you with the knowledge and tools to confidently take the next steps in your personal and professional life.

Full disclaimer: this book is a collection of real-life stories, experiences, and insights. It is not designed to be a full-on playbook. It is meant to be a mirror. I am an avid believer that you don't attract what you want, you attract who you are. Following that belief, you'll naturally be attracted to chapters and authors that, in some way, shape, or form mirror aspects of yourself.

(RE)INTRODUCTION

But, before I get too far into the introduction of this book, allow me to (re)introduce myself! My name is Chantée Christian, your official "Ambassador of Awareness" on this expedition. *Throughout this introduction and my chapter, cultural nods will be running rampant—consider it my personal touch.* I am a catalyst for growth, change, and inspired action. As a catalyst, I've navigated experiences that not only shape my understanding of self but also illuminate how I can contribute to the growth and well-being of others.

RADICAL AWARENESS

Embarking on my journey of "radical awareness," I found myself in countless situations to practice what I preach. What do I mean? Well, I'm notorious for emphasizing the dual nature of a growth mindset. The first part involves learning and absorbing knowledge—the most commonly visited portion of a growth mindset. However, true growth and expansion reside in the second part—applying what you've learned. It's similar to the pressure that turns coal into diamonds, a transformative process that unfolds in those pivotal moments where we reveal our true selves.

Some wise person on the good Beyoncé internet once said that our prayers to God are akin to calling Him, and His response manifests as our intuition. If this holds true, let me share how I almost missed the call, symbolizing this very moment.

In October/November 2020, I was presented with the opportunity to contribute to my first book, **Leading Through the Pandemic: Unconventional Wisdom from Heartfelt Leaders.** I did so without fully grasping the impact it would have on my life—initially, at least. It wasn't until people started reaching out and expressing their thoughts on my chapter that I began to comprehend the profound effect it was having. People shared how they saw themselves in my words or were delighted to discover a part of me they hadn't known. Fast forward a few months, and my second book was released, and people said they loved it even more. This got me thinking—there's something special about this communal approach to sharing and amplifying voices.

One night, the phrase "Awareness Put Me On" echoed in my mind. In true Chantée fashion, I started singing Jeezy's "I put on for my city..." and thought, "That's a dope title for something." Weeks later, the phrase resurfaced, and this time, I wrote it down in one of my notebooks. I began to ask myself questions, jot down hooks, names of potential authors, a preferred publisher, and the overall vibe of the book—I firmly believe in writing things down and making them plain! Recently, I heard that writing it down and making it plain isn't just for you; it's for the people joining you on the journey.

I closed that notebook and went about my life as usual. However, nearly three years later, I found myself in tears in front of a close coach friend, expressing my frustration and unsure of what to do. I kept asking God for guidance, feeling like He had forgotten me or couldn't hear me. I remember her response so clearly. She said, "He has already given you the answer. You have to make a move so He can make a move. Stop asking Him for something He has already given you." Let's just say I was crying even harder. Even though I didn't fully believe it in that moment...I felt it.

I learned a long time ago that you don't have to believe something to be true. The two are not mutually exclusive. I gathered myself, considering we were at a retreat and on a working break. While walking to get a drink (*non-alcoholic; however, I felt like an alcoholic one was warranted, but I digress*), an attendee asked if I could help her incorporate more of herself into her own book. We sat down and had a conversation. Out of genuine interest, I asked questions while she openly shared her thoughts. It felt great, and she was able to leave with a recording of her honest reflections during our conversation. Being of service to people is one of my realizations about myself. This interaction reminded me of what God had told me. Rushing to my room to see if, for some odd chance, I had that particular notebook with me. And I did. It's still unclear why I had it with me at the time since it only had five blank pages left in it, but I digress! Flipping to the page where I had written "Awareness Put Me On" and all the details, I immediately became keenly aware that I couldn't sit on this project any longer—not another minute, not another year!

LEADING BY CHOICE OR BY DEFAULT?

As your "Ambassador of Awareness" on this enlightenment journey, I encourage you to think about how you are currently leading in your personal and professional life. Are you leading by choice or by default? Remember, who you are in one space is who you are in all spaces. It may manifest or look differently depending on the environment.

Alright! Everyone on board! Get ready for a transformative adventure as we dive into the pages of *Awareness Put Me On*. Curated by a diverse group of people, this book invites you to explore how heightened awareness not only transforms lives –it also ignites profound change! These stories uncover pivotal moments when heightened awareness served as a catalyst for transformative shifts.

This isn't your run-of-the-mill leadership book. We've meticulously cultivated a space where leaders felt at ease sharing beyond the surface-level narratives that have cluttered bookshelves (no shade intended). The authors dug deep to ensure you could feel seen, heard, motivated, inspired and reassured that you're not alone. In the words of Brené Brown, "You can't get to courage without rumbling with vulnerability." Let me assure you that the courage exhibited by these authors throughout this book is unparalleled! As Naval Ravikant perfectly put it, "To write a great book, you must first become the book." These authors embody that sentiment.

I invite you to be active participants in your own transformation. Here's your assignment should you choose to accept it:

1. **Engage Authentically:** Dive into the stories with an open heart.
2. **Personalize Your Experience:** Use Post-it notes, a highlighter, or any method that allows you to flag things that speak to you.
3. **Redefine Leadership:** Understand that leadership starts with you.
4. **Amplify Your Presence:** Ask yourself, "What would it look like for you to amplify your presence in your spheres of leadership and personal development?"

Think of this as more than an anthology; it's an invitation to be the change you want to see and witness your own metamorphosis. It's an opportunity to amplify your voice in various spaces of leadership and personal development.

Remember, the power of awareness is not just within the words on these pages; it's in the application of the insights in your own life. Embrace the journey, and let this book be your compass toward a life of (increased) purpose, authenticity, and meaningful growth.

Let this book be a conversation starter. Share your thoughts, favorite passages, and insights with others. Let the dialogue extend beyond these pages and ripple into your communities.

Are you ready to lead by choice and thrive by design?

Let's get into it!

PART I

PERSONAL DEVELOPMENT

"The answers keep unfolding as your life expands, if you're willing to see things for what they are—and what they can be."

— OPRAH WINFREY

1

CHARLOTTE R. JACOBS, MBA, PCC, CPC, ELI-MP

GETTING OUT OF MY OWN WAY

I am an encourager—an advocate for others. If you come to me with an issue that you feel you just can't seem to move past, I'm the one who will guide and support you through the darkness. You know those times when you have to move a mountain, but you don't know how? That's how I help. When my close friend reached out, she was in the depths of hopelessness about her future and uncertain about her direction. It seemed like she had hit a dead end in her career, and the enthusiasm she once had was nowhere to be found. However, after our conversation, a surge of energy transformed her outlook. The excitement that sparked within her was contagious, and I, too, felt invigorated by the positive shift in her perspective. After our conversation, my friend's transformation was not just palpable but electrifying, turning a bleak situation into a beacon of potential and excitement. After our conversation, she felt energized and so did I.

I have been a leadership coach for over two decades, working with organizations across the United States and in Europe. I can successfully identify and outline behaviors that negatively impact performance and show their correlation. Coaching is my niche, but it was not something I ever thought I could do. I never imagined I would stand in front of senior leaders reporting on performance areas needing improvement. You see, I was part of society's statistical data and census report that said because I came from a single-parent home, I would have limitations in life that would prevent me from contributing to society. And that, my friend, is the beginning of my self-sabotaging beliefs.

Self-sabotage is a form of self-negation or self-depreciation. People of Color (POC) often face unique challenges and societal pressures, which can contribute to them internalizing negative stereotypes and self-doubt. Understanding self-sabotage and its consequences is essential for promoting healing and empowerment within the POC community. Self-sabotage refers to the unconscious or conscious process of doubting or undermining your abilities, qualities, and worth.

During my tenure as a dealer support associate at a mutual funds company, I grappled with a sense of impostor syndrome. My self-imposed limitations led me to believe I was inferior to my colleagues, convincing me that my thoughts were not valuable enough to voice. As I persisted in this role, a journey of self-discovery unfolded. I came to recognize that my behavior was influenced by deep-seated issues, including low self-esteem, internalized racism, and a persistent need for external validation. I observed instances where I refrained from correcting or addressing inaccurate statements in performance reviews, and I often found myself shrinking away in moments of confrontation. This realization marked the beginning of a profound journey towards understanding and addressing these underlying factors in order to foster personal growth and authenticity.

I've carried the invisible luggage around, filled with limiting beliefs. I am not good enough. I will not be successful. No one will listen to me. There is no need to try because I will not be successful. I am a female in a male-dominated world, and I know your place. Be seen and not heard. You are a minority that will have a glass ceiling lower than others. **YOU ARE NOT GOOD ENOUGH.**

Picture the heaviness of lugging around that emotional baggage, a load that only intensified as I navigated through life's journey. It became utterly draining. I felt the weight on my shoulders, a persistent exhaustion that permeated my entire being. My days were overshadowed by a constant refrain of "I can't." I found myself steering clear of valuable speaking engagements and networking opportunities, potentially paving the way for personal growth and happiness, were routinely dismissed. I was convinced that I didn't deserve happiness. The root of this belief traced back to a hurtful comment made by an elementary school teacher who predicted I wouldn't amount to anything. It's like a punch in the gut every time I think about it — a bubble buster of epic proportions.

Yet, there was a fire burning deep within me—an insatiable itch that demanded attention. I yearned to break free from the confines of the label I had been assigned and explore uncharted territories. My heart pulsated with a desire to see more, do more, and become more. The quaint town of Suffolk, Virginia, known for Mr. Peanut, couldn't contain the dreams swelling within me. I envisioned a life filled with continuous learning and forging connections with new faces. Determined, I decided to embark on a journey to explore the vast expanse of our world. My aim was clear – to make both my earthly and heavenly family proud. Mediocrity was never in my destiny; I was crafted for greatness, destined to be a catalyst for change. A dream burned brightly within me, fueling my passion and determination to shape lives.

My teenage years were a balance of the best and the worst. I come from a large, close-knit family. We loved and protected each other. Mess with one, you mess with all. We shared good times by entertaining each other or playing games. But then there was the worst. Can we keep the running water on? What will we eat? How will we stay warm? My mother did her best to protect us from household problems. She put on a brave face and supported the family by working multiple jobs. She was determined to have a better life. Her goal was to give her children a head start in life, one different from what she had. Seeing my mother's drive and determination was the catalyst that made me determined to want more. And so it began: the desire not to be a product of my environment but to take those obstacles and make them stepping stones to reach my goals.

After graduating high school, I could not afford college, so I worked local jobs from cashier to newspaper delivery. One day, my life changed while I was working at an athletic store. Two professionally dressed men came in to look around. Before leaving, they approached me. They began by apologizing for seeming weird, but they had a job offer. They needed a secretary for their office, and they saw something in me. Me, I thought? Who walks into a store and then offers a stranger a job? Not just a job, but a good job! After asking for some time to think about it and discuss it with family and friends, I decided to take a leap of faith, and I said yes. I now have my first professional job! This opportunity gave me confidence. I was on my way to fulfilling my goals.

Over the next several years, I continued working but wanted more. I enjoyed meeting new and different people in a professional atmosphere. I loved the diversity of the customers, and to meet new people and improve my future prospects, I enrolled in a community college to take a few classes. I was deeply curious to learn more about the world. But even though there was a high level of excitement, there was also the belief that I would not be successful in college. I would eventually fail because I did not deserve this opportunity. However, I was determined to succeed and would not give up. And I did not give up. This experience was what I needed and more to drive my goals.

My job changed over the next couple of years, and I found myself at a mutual funds firm. I was excited to experience this level of corporate, but my time here tested my faith and belief. It was here that I had my first encounter with racism and bias against me as an African-American woman. Nothing I did was right; it was always subpar. My personal time and attendance were micromanaged. I was held accountable for things my peers were overlooked for.

Despite the pain I was feeling, someone came in who would completely change my life.

Enter my coworker, Denise. Denise is a die-hard African-American woman from New York who was responsible for training me. Through a test of her patience and sanity, I was successfully onboarded. Over time our relationship as coworkers blossomed into a beautiful friendship that still exists to this day. During my time at this firm, I watched how Denise professionally handled many attempts to scrutinize her and the work she performed, but she did not allow it. She addressed every accusation with tact and intent. She corrected misunderstandings and false assumptions. For one of the first times, I saw a woman articulate and engage with leaders with ease. And I admired her for that. I was shown how to have a voice and how to use it. I began to speak up more and address attempts to intimidate me. But I also learned the importance of holding myself accountable for my actions. I had to be responsible for the controllables, so I began to self-evaluate myself. I began to understand my part in each situation and then created action plans to prevent the mistake from occurring again. The skills I learned from Denise allowed me to pivot in another role, where my love for coaching began.

Denise often teases me about my dramatic exit from the job at the mutual funds firm. If you can believe it, I decided to resign right in the middle of a meeting! Although I was frightened, it was something I had begun to prepare for emotionally and financially. And so I began a new journey with more clarity about my professional goals, and a deeper awareness about the person I aim to be. As I transitioned into my new career at a start-up company, I was quickly promoted to the role of manager within three months. I purchased my first home and enrolled in an HBCU, something I never thought would happen. Within six years, I was a top-performing leader, known for driving results in several business units. As I approached my eighth year, I worked full-time and completed my MBA. I also obtained another position as a leadership coach that granted me an opportunity I had only dreamt of—to travel throughout the US and Europe.

With each new journey, comes new obstacles. As an executive leader, I was now interacting with a new group of people with new demands. I had to be more proactive to get what I needed, and now I had more responsibility to hold others accountable for their work. There were times when I was challenged, and I began to question my abilities, wondering if I was capable of being successful. I began to fall back into the mindset of doubting myself, telling myself I was not worthy. Even though I had accomplished so much over the years, I still felt unworthy and began to self-sabotage. I began to overthink and question my work. I began to strive for perfection – if it was not near perfection, it was not ready to share or present. My mental and emotional health began to suffer as my stress and anxiety increased. I isolated myself from friends and family, choosing to stay alone and bathe in pity. I was suffering, and so was my work. I had to find a way, my way, to move forward. I needed to renew my faith in myself and my abilities. I needed a shift, and it came.

A pivotal moment for me that was life-changing was the awareness that I was not taking full responsibility for my actions. I suffered from low self-esteem and doubted my abilities. I was self-sabotaging myself in my daily life. I was using past experiences as obstacles to being a victim. My limiting beliefs were holding me back from my destiny, and it was time for me to make changes. To move forward, I took accountability and responsibility for what I owned. I created an action plan to break the cycle of self-sabotaging. My plan began with taking eight intentional steps to live purposely and authentically.

Identify the behavior. I had to be honest with myself about my part. I had to recognize what I was doing that created the cycle of self-sabotaging. This meant admitting that I was on a downward path to self-destruction. People of Color, in particular, should engage in self-reflection and introspection to uncover the underlying beliefs and messages that contribute to self-sabotage. This may involve examining personal experiences, cultural narratives, and media messages that reinforce negative stereotypes.

Practice accountability and responsibility. No change can occur without taking accountability and responsibility for my actions. Avoiding these actions would make it impossible to create new habits to break the cycle. Challenge and reject stereotypes that perpetuate self-sabotage. I did this through education, activism, and engaging with diverse communities that promote inclusivity and acceptance.

Recognize my trigger points. Self-sabotaging stems from limiting beliefs, assumptions, and fears. Identifying my triggers helps me to understand why I felt and acted the way I did. I realized that my procrastination was a form of self-sabotaging because of my fear of failure and judgment. POC should

Remove judgment and self-doubt. Self-sabotaging can be fueled by negative thinking. By practicing self-love, I can break the cycle of guilt and self-blame. Look for opportunities to engage in activities that promote self-care, set boundaries, and seek support from trusted individuals or support groups.

Create an action plan to move forward. By not setting realistic goals, I set myself up for failure. It was important to have a methodology that worked so I used SMART goals. (Specific. Measurable. Attainable. Realistic. Time- focused).

Surround myself with positive and encouraging people. The saying "birds of a feather flock together" could not be further from the truth. If you surround yourself with people who only see the worst in situations, always complain or are never positive, you will eventually take on that mindset. Instead, find your circle of family members and friends that will keep you on track and encourage you. As I was writing my chapter in this book, my dear friend Wardell called to check on my progress. I was feeling ashamed because I was behind, but Wardell reminded me that I could do this. He took the time to strategize with me, giving me suggestions and topics to consider. He believes in me, and he put me back on track to completing my chapter.

Give myself grace. How can I believe in the Almighty and not have faith? I was not created as a human to be perfect. Making mistakes is a part of my journey. Those mistakes allowed me to learn and grow, to move and not become stagnant. The self-hate I experienced were roadblocks to distract me, and they did… just for a brief moment until I realized and remembered for me to succeed, I had to get comfortable being uncomfortable. I incorporated good habits such as exercising and spending more time with those I loved into my daily routine.

Re-assess and re-engage. Take time to evaluate what was achieved compared to my goal. What was working for me? What was not? What am I willing to continue doing? What will I change to continue moving towards my goal?

I've come to realize that self-sabotage is a pervasive issue that affects the well-being of people of color. We can create a more inclusive and equitable society by understanding its consequences and promoting strategies to overcome self-sabotage. It is crucial for people of color to recognize and challenge the negative stereotypes that perpetuate self-sabotage, build self-esteem, and seek professional help when needed.

As a woman of color, my vision for the future is brimming with hope and dreams that transcend any self-sabotaging beliefs. I see a path ahead where my identity is not a limitation but a source of strength and empowerment. In this future, I envision breaking through barriers and dismantling systemic obstacles, creating opportunities for not only myself but for others in my community. My dreams include a world where diversity is celebrated, and individuals of all backgrounds are given equal chances to thrive. By discarding self-limiting beliefs, I am crafting a narrative of resilience, determination, and success, paving the way for a brighter and more inclusive tomorrow.

ABOUT THE AUTHOR

Charlotte Jacobs is a globally recognized Executive Leadership Coach and Organizational Strategist. She partners with clients to discover how to INVEST the necessary time, energy and resources needed to LEAD the lives and careers they are meant to. She has over 20 years of specialized experience as a coach, consultant, facilitator, and trainer. She has implemented cost-reducing leadership coaching and performance-based reward programs in corporations throughout the US and Europe. She is the founder and CEO of InvestNLead, LLC, a coaching and consulting group, and is also an Executive Leadership Coach for a Fortune 500 company. She is a Professional Certified Coach (PCC) credentialed through the International Coaching Federation (ICF), a graduate of the John Maxwell Coach Training program and is an Energy Leader Index-Master Practitioner.

Charlotte is active on several boards to include the International Coaching Federation (ICF) Virginia Board as the DEIB Director. She obtained a bachelor's degree from Hampton University, an MBA from Averett University and holds several certifications. She is a proud member of Delta Sigma Theta Sorority, Inc. Charlotte lives by her motto: Your desire to want to change has to be greater than your comfort to stay the same. With this motto, she has helped clients identify obstacles invading their journey towards the happiness they deserve.

2

CHANTÉE L. CHRISTIAN

CEASE-AND-DESIST THE INTERNAL BS

"...because if we remember, God doesn't make mistakes, and if He called you into that position no matter how overwhelming the position, that's because He believes you're the woman for the job. So then our ask to God is what is it that you know about me to place me in this position? 'Cause if you placed me in this position, you know something about me that I don't know yet..."

— SARAH JAKES ROBERTS

Excuse me? Excuse me, Jesus?! Uhhh…may I speak to your manager? I think I received the wrong order. Yes, I need YOUR manager. I would like a FULL refund! This is NOT the life I was expecting. I can't believe this is what you gave me. OHHH…He is busy, WOW…OK, I'll wait! I got time today!

After waiting for the manager for more than an hour with no answer, I scream into my pillow, "GOD, WHY?!?! SEND ME HELP! Can't you see me in distress? LOOK at what your people have done!" As I anxiously pace back and forth, my mind begins to swirl with all sorts of scenarios.

I find myself asking, where is my help?! Well, why would it come? People don't know what is *really* going on. I have been so caught up in *not* complaining that I refrained from sharing the severity of my mental and physical exhaustion. A lot of people think I am the epitome of strength and having my shit together (spoiler alert – that perception couldn't be any further from the truth). Yes, having an award-winning podcast and a TV show are pretty big deals. Yet, these societal makers of success have distorted some people's perceptions of me.

People assume my life has been a bed of roses because of what they see on social media. The truth of the matter is my life is just as chaotic and full of ups and downs as the next person. I am human, no one has it all together. Even in all the chaos, I attribute the preservation of my sanity to God, coaching, therapy, bourbon, whiskey, and a great network of people around me.

RE(INTRODUCTION)

Allow me to re-introduce myself, my name is Chantée Christian. AND, I am in recovery. Not the kind of recovery you are probably thinking, but the kind that is essential for growth and expansion. I am on a complex healing journey. I am a recovering: (1) people pleaser; (2) overachiever; (3) strong Black woman; (4) perfectionist; (5) approval seeker; (6) overthinker; (7) validation seeker…and about a million more.

Throughout this chapter, you'll hear me talk to God like a friend. Because we are friends, at least in my mind, and that's all that matters! I will also likely curse. I mean – just look at the title of my chapter.

This chapter wasn't going to be heavy on my faith, and yet here we are. Faith is so intricately woven into the fabric of my being. After all, I am Christian squared. Get it?!? For the people pulling up the rear, my last name is Christian, and I am a Christian. *I'll give you a minute to go back and laugh…because that was hilarious.*

Alright, we've got all the preliminary stuff out of the way.

Are you ready to take a trip down memory lane?!? Buckle up!

Let's GO!

BACK IN THE DAYS – WHEN I WAS YOUNG...I'M NOT A KID ANYMORE

As a kid I would often find myself in trouble for what my parents amusingly dubbed "feeding the neighborhood." I saw it as a way of sharing with others, an instinctual act of kindness. I wasn't fully aware of how my parents perceived it—they viewed it as an attempt to fit in and they were not amused with my distribution of their groceries around the neighborhood. As an adult, I can see where they were coming from. If every time I went into the freezer for a **Push UP** or **Rocket** popsicle and there were none, I'd be aggravated, too! Groceries are expensive!

However, if they had come from a space of curiosity, they would have realized that my intentions were not to "fit in." I found true fulfillment in helping and giving to others—a concept I've since recognized as being an act of service. I thrived on the opportunity to be of assistance.

When asked what I wanted to be when I grew up, I would say, a lawyer and then I shifted to a teacher. As life would have it, I didn't become a lawyer. I do teach, not in a traditional way, though. It took years of investing time, money, and resources to understand that my assignments, like "feeding the neighborhood," were actually preparing me to walk in my purpose.

DON'T WALK AWAY

I often talk about my (former) dream of climbing the corporate ladder and settling into a rather cozy life. I was cruising along that path until BAM – the global pandemic! Life threw the world a curveball. While many consider the first year of the pandemic a nightmare, rightfully so. It was a horrific time for many. For me, 2020 to 2022 turned out to be some of the most transformative years, both personally and professionally. It was finally a chance for me to pause and reassess what truly mattered in my life. I had been so focused on serving others that I had stunted my own growth and dreams.

No matter how hard I hit the pause button on my inner thoughts and feelings, there was an undeniable urge nudging me to take action. Being accustomed to ignoring such thoughts, I initially let them sit and marinate. In 2020, a series of events unfolded one after the other, leading me to an understanding that I was on assignment, and if I didn't move with a sense of urgency, I was going to miss a prime opportunity to live out my purpose.

Let me back up and explain what I mean. For me, the biggest differentiator is that you can do an assignment without truly challenging your own beliefs or making sacrifices. However, with a purpose, or as some would say, a calling, you often find yourself wrestling with doubts and fears that stem from various sources (i.e., insecurity, external pressures, etc.).

I found myself wrestling with thoughts that were literally paralyzing me. I was too afraid to take a step. I was filled with a fear that I would lose everything because I went against the grain. The major turning point came when I was deeply unsettled and disappointed by how my company responded to George Floyd's murder and its aftermath. It was keeping me up at night, and I couldn't shake the words of my dad, "Don't complain about something if you aren't willing to put in the work to change it." So, I proposed an idea to my now creative director: a panel discussion titled "Unspoken Truths of Being Black in the Workforce." Initially, I was confident about the concept, but as I drove home that night, doubt crept in. What had I gotten myself into? Who would come? Who did I think I was?

Talking to one of my coaches, I admitted my fears that no one would show up and that I could jeopardize my job and reputation trying to prove a point. When she asked me why I wanted to do this, I realized I needed a moment to gather my thoughts. I returned with a renewed sense of purpose—to encourage self-expression and leadership, even if only one person walked away with valuable insights. With that clarity, I knew there was no turning back, even if doubts still lingered in the back of my mind. God wouldn't put it on my heart to abandon me. Right?

99 PROBLEMS

I organized, hosted, and moderated over a dozen amazing panel discussions called *Unspoken Truths of Being Black*, addressing crucial topics like the workforce, healthcare, and education in the context of heightened awareness amidst the global pandemic and racial injustice. I'm proud to say the entire series won an award in the category of diversity, equity, and inclusion. *Unspoken Truths* served as the kickstarter to my podcast, *My Best SHIFT*, which also won an award that same year.

However, no one prepared me to navigate both an out-of-body excitement coupled with extreme sadness for what used to be. Working with a therapist and a few coaches, I was able to clearly identify the stages of grief I was going through. I hadn't felt such deep feelings of confusion, scary darkness, and sadness since one of my aunts and little cousins died in a car accident due to a drunk driver.

Something about the sudden losses that altered my ability to accept a multitude of *truths* in my life. Unfortunately, my mind had been processing all of the amazing accomplishments as losses because they weren't how I had imagined my life would be.

Well, let me tell you…I sure as hell didn't sign up for that! I did not sign up for grieving who I used to be; what I used to do, and who I was…a fraud! The mind is a chaotic place at times. In my mind, I wasn't worthy of accolades and success. So, I would say things to God that I knew better than to say.

Picture it: Washington, D.C., summer of 2022, a beautiful sunny day, birds chirping, and the kids playing outside. Me and my friend, God, chit chatting as we often do. And I BOLDLY say to Him, "Even if everything with this project (TV show) fails…you know goes to hell in a handbasket, I want to be able to learn something new."

God said…OH, you want to learn. Let me teach you.

JESUS TAKE THE WHEEL

From October 2022 until January 2024, the lessons were beyond anything I could have imagined! I've never called on God and Jesus so much in my life. For most of 2023, night after night, tears would soak my pillow, only for me to wake up and face the same overwhelming challenges that seemed to be weighing me down – with a smile.

One day, a friend reached out, and as I spilled out all the chaos in my life – dried-up contracts, empty bank accounts, the added stress of a new car, a TV show launch looming, and a massive release party in the works – it all seemed insurmountable.

I felt so inadequate. How could I be a coach, an advocate, and an expert when my own life was in shambles?! It seemed like every time I managed to get one aspect of my life in order, another would come crashing down. It felt like I couldn't find stable ground like I was destined to move to 444 Shambleville Express Way!

To the outside world, I appeared normal, cheerful, the life of the party. But in reality, I was barely holding it together, giving just enough to keep from collapsing from exhaustion, sadness, and illness. I was angry at God, feeling like He had led me astray.

Despite my reluctance to return to corporate life, my attempts at finding alternative income sources, even through Instacart, left me feeling defeated. I'll never forget standing in that international market, tears streaming down my face as I struggled to read the signs, all for $38.08. Not even enough to fill my tank! It felt like a divine intervention when I heard God asking, "WHAT ARE YOU DOING!?"

That same friend reminded me that entrepreneurship is NOT for the faint of heart. He continually asked me how dedicated I was to my company and what was I willing to do to keep it afloat. He asked me if I had exhausted all my options. I thought I had, but deep down, we both knew I had hit a (creative, inspirational, motivational) wall. With the support of a few friends, him included, I revamped my resume and hit the job market once again, only to be met with a barrage of rejection letters. Oddly enough, each rejection felt like a blessing in disguise. If any of those companies had said yes, we might not have this empowering movement of awareness and conscious leadership. Without a doubt, I would have shelved my purpose in order to fulfill someone else's assignment for me. I will tell anyone that there are so many blessings in the no. It isn't easy to hear or receive, but when the yes finally comes. WHEW! That level of appreciation and relief is undeniable.

Let's keep it 100 – my ego took a HUGE beating. And if I'm completely honest, my feelings were hurt. How could they not pick me?! I'm overqualified. I could do these jobs in my sleep. AND yet, I could hear that little voice in my head saying, "See you weren't all that" or "It's okay you couldn't do that job anyway" or "You've been gone too long." Those thoughts did a number on me. I worked my ass off with my wellness community and friend group to reprogram my mind and my heart.

A constant prayer I prayed was for Jesus to be a fence to shield me from my enemies, failing to recognize that I was my own worst adversary. I had gotten rather cozy with disobedience.

COZY

What have you gotten cozy with lately? And no, I'm not talking about a book, a glass of wine, or your favorite blanket. I mean, what mindset and agreements have you gotten cozy with?

I'll go first. I had gotten cozy with a couple of things. One was, "I got it." The coziness with "I got it" led me to build walls of shame around what was really happening in my bank accounts. So much so that when I FINALLY disclosed my financial woes to my partner, I cried uncontrollably, believing he would leave because I didn't have it anymore. The truth was that he was far more understanding, kind, and supportive than I was to myself.

Another was "faith without works is dead." Before you come after me, please let me explain. I think when a lot of us heard and/or were taught that saying we took it as we have to work hard in order to activate our faith. And after my 40-plus years on this earth, I disagree. I think the key isn't hard work in the way we thought. I think the "works" that are referred to can be summarized in this equation: obedience + sacrifice = reward + favor. In order to be obedient, you must sacrifice something. It can be your ego, the need to be right, or anything that is a sacrifice for you to fully reap the reward and favor that is attached to it.

People say, favor isn't fair, but they don't know what you had to let go of to gain that favor. It is WORK! It is belief and truly getting comfortable enough with God to ask Him…show me why you chose me? I don't see it yet, but I know you called me here for a reason. Help me see it and remove any blocks or resistance so that I can **MOVE**.

STEP ASIDE

Two days before the *All The Ships TV* show launch party, my biggest sponsor backed out. Normally, I would have been a wreck, but oddly enough, I was calm. When my publicist/friend called the next morning with potential solutions, I calmly said, "We aren't changing anything. It'll work itself out. I'm going back to my praise and worship. I'll talk to you later." She probably thought I'd lost my mind, and truthfully, I wondered the same. As a program manager, by nature, it would only make sense for me to ruminate with her on different ideas and strategies.

Walking into the party, I knew I didn't have all the money to pay for the venue. I can't deny that it was heavy on my mind. The fear of the card being declined terrified me. As fate would have it, I was walking up the stairs as a friend was walking down. He stopped and asked me what was wrong. My immediate reaction was nothing! I have been smiling all day. He said, "I know you; something is wrong." I told him what was plaguing my mind. And he said, "Tell them to bring me the bill, and I'll take care of it." Through my tears, I said something to the effect of having to work the red-light district to pay him back, and we both laughed, and he said, "I got you."

It wasn't that he paid the remaining balance, although I will be forever grateful. It was the first time in my life, I didn't have my hands in what God was working on. I wasn't trying to control the outcome and getting wildly worked up over things I couldn't change. I realized that God didn't need my help. And because I wasn't in the helping business, He was able to provide for me in a way that I could have never.

Despite feeling spiritually aligned, my external situation hadn't improved. In fact, it had worsened. Even so, I stopped saying the year was grade-A trash and that I wanted a **FULL** refund on it. I know that our beliefs are thoughts that we continue to believe. So, if you want to change your beliefs, change your thoughts.

I recognized that these experiences were giving me exactly what I asked for. I was heavy in a learning season. Pastor Sheryl Brady talks about an instance when she was disappointed and frustrated that a *door* had closed, and she said she heard God say to her, "I am the man in your life, I will open all the doors." I inserted step aside. I remember, as a kid, my dad would tap my hand when I would reach for the door and not step aside so that he could open the door. Hearing that reinforced my commitment to stepping aside. I had to divorce the idea of controlling my life and instead embrace the concept of stepping aside and letting God guide me.

I realized that God was the ultimate manager, orchestrating every moment of my life, not me. Silencing my mind is me telling it to cease and desist on the internal BS because I know I am the right person. This is my time. I've paid my dues. I'm thinking the right thoughts. I'm doing the right things. At this very moment, I'm where I'm supposed to be…in position for the greatest breakthrough ever.

Because I remember that God doesn't make mistakes.

ABOUT THE AUTHOR

Chantée L. Christian is a two-time international best-selling author, the founder of My Best SHIFT and CC Media, the host of *Unspoken Truths of Being Black*, and a TV producer and host of *All the Ships*.

Chantée is the driving force behind My Best SHIFT, an innovative coaching and consulting company and an award-winning podcast where she helps leaders shift their mindset to take inspired action. Chantée is the host and moderator of the award-winning conversational series *Unspoken Truths of Being Black*, addressing crucial topics like the workforce, healthcare, and education in the context of heightened awareness.

With over two decades in management consulting, Chantée has specialized in Program/Project Management, Organizational Change Management, and Strategic Planning. As a certified facilitator, Chantée has developed and delivered diverse training programs for staff at all levels. She received her Bachelor's degree from George Mason University and a Masters of Business Administration from Webster University.

Chantée is also a 2021 Northern Virginia 40 Under 40 honoree. Her diverse background, combined with her extensive certifications and professional achievements, positions her as a dynamic leader across industries.

Growing up as an Army brat, Chantée has developed a passion for exploration and travel. One of her favorite forms of exploration is through food. Another form of exploration Chantée includes her musical sanctuary. It is an invitation to a great time with artists ranging from Whitney Houston to Cardi B., and a plethora of artists in between like Klymaxx, Babyface, Jezzy, Maverick City Music, Ed Sheeran, Adele, and Beyonce. Understanding Chantée means recognizing her pure delight for stationary, music, delectable cuisine, getaways, and laughter!

https://mybestshift.buzzsprout.com/

3

CHENISE UPSHUR

CHASING PEACE

It was early 2021. The clock struck six A.M., and my alarm was blaring. I rolled over, hit snooze, and waited for it to begin blaring again. I didn't want to get out of bed. I didn't want to get out of bed so bad that anything in the world sounded better than getting up and starting my day. Even a root canal sounded more appealing at that moment. As I lay in bed for those eight minutes between the first ring of my alarm clock and the second inevitable one, I wished I were anywhere but there. I wished I would get hit by a truck. I didn't want to die, I just wanted to rest, relax, not be needed, and not feel like the weight of everyone else was on my shoulders.

As I sit here from my current space of peace, I can't even pinpoint what set me over the edge. I had a good job, family and friends who loved me, and what others would consider a "good life." The reality, though, was that I had been living with a weight for years. It had been added ounce by ounce, and that morning, I finally crumbled under a load I could no longer bear. I now define peace as a space where my mind is quiet. A moment in time unhampered by the guilt and reflection of yesterday or the concern and anxiety for tomorrow. Peace is a moment in time when you are completely content in the present, and the past and future do not exist. It took me a while to come to this definition. As I began running from feelings and emotions I no longer wanted to claim, I needed to define what I wanted to run to, find, and ultimately create for myself.

WOW, THAT'S A BIG "AHA MOMENT"

Most people think of awareness as these wonderful "aha moments"–moments where a bright light shines down, and an amazing transformation takes place. My story is the exact opposite. My awareness came from one of the deepest, darkest places I've ever been. My "aha moment" came when I realized how far away from peace I was and that I was willing to do anything to define and find peace for myself. There have been a lot of great moments since 2021, but none of them would have happened without the depths of despair, depression, and anxiety that I found myself in at six A.M. that early 2021.

Thankfully, my son had to go to school; it was the only reason I finally got out of bed that morning. When I returned home, I sat down and tried to gauge why being comatose in the hospital sounded better than the current version of my life. I was drained. Not just the "I need a spa day" kind of drained, but the kind where you have poured out your heart, soul, and very life reserves in you, and there is nothing left to give. My inability to set boundaries, realize my own limitations, and articulate what I wanted had created a version of myself that I hated. I felt disconnected and disjointed. It was as though people needed different versions of me and I had fractured myself into multiple versions to meet the needs of those around me.

The different versions included leader, mom, friend, sibling, co-worker, and confidante to name a few, and I couldn't get these pieces back together to create a whole. In the corporate world, the phrase that comes to mind is "bringing your whole self." In my focus to be everything for everyone, I was the complete antithesis of that phrase. I had always presented myself as a whole person and did so with integrity and genuineness. I was so disconnected that I had become completely blind to how I felt and who I was. I was surprised at how much guilt and shame surrounded that realization. I felt guilty that I had done this to myself and ashamed that I had unknowingly lied not only to others but myself for so many years. I had no clue how to become "whole," but I knew I had to do something different.

I should have been pouring into myself by engaging in new experiences and reflecting on how those experiences created emotions and new perspectives in me. Instead, I was using my heart, soul, and life reserves to fuel the multiple leadership positions I held and the development programs I ran without any acknowledgment that the reserves were finite. While pouring so much of myself into those programs and positions, I was doing nothing to develop myself. The very same day I graduated from Vanderbilt University in 2008, my grandfather asked when I was going to apply for my master's. I remember feeling like I had just achieved a major academic milestone, and my job was complete. While my grandfather celebrated my current accomplishments, he knew what I didn't understand until over ten years later. He knew that people who give of themselves need to be maniacal in their focus to have something to give. While his words frustrated me in the moment, looking back I can't thank him enough for the love and care he offered.

Flash forward to 2021, and I did ultimately decide to apply for a master's program to reignite my love of learning. Feeling empty, drained, and with nothing left to give, I had better find a source to fill me up fast. That one action ended up changing my whole life. Immediately, I realized how much I missed actively learning. For as long as I can remember, my mantra was to learn something new and teach something new every day. I had never stopped looking to pick up nuggets of knowledge and wisdom, but the structured approach to learning and self-development was a fuel I hadn't realized I needed. I was overwhelmed by the positive response from people around me to my excitement of learning. They could tell that learning was fueling me and wanted to help fan that fire. I ended up being nominated for two separate year-long corporate development programs that kicked off in 2022.

People continuously asked if I had too much on my plate going into 2022. I was starting the second term of my master's program, was part of two separate year-long corporate development programs, and had a pretty demanding full-time job managing coaches and developing them into managers. On top of that, I was a single mom. It was a lot, but I had to do everything in my power to keep away that level of despair that was felt that fateful morning in 2021. I could deal with busyness, deadlines, and more plates in the air than I care to count, but I knew I couldn't deal with that feeling again. I still hadn't put a definition to the word "peace," but I knew there had to be something different, something better, and so I was maniacal in my focus to find it.

By focusing on myself, I began naming and stripping away all the learnings, habits, and damaged parts that no longer served me. I remember talking with a friend one afternoon and finally admitting how much the statement from my parents, "You are the oldest. You need to set the bar for your siblings," was impacting me. As the eldest of ten kids, the belief that my actions, successes, failures, and goals in life directly impacted nine others was a cancer that had eaten away at my psyche for years. Not only my siblings but cousins, friends, new people at work, and even my son factored into this deep-rooted belief inside of me. I remember thinking back over decisions I had made based on the impressions that they would make on others, and realizing those decisions didn't benefit me. Actually, they didn't always benefit the other person either. This allowed me to focus on what I needed on my journey to be a whole person, and that was a new feeling. This was only one of the old mindsets discarded on my way to addressing what no longer served me

You can be so much more when you have less weight weighing you down. The container that holds the memories, emotions, beliefs, and learning that makes you "you" can only hold so much. When I looked inside that container and into my very being, the majority of my capacity was filled with trash. I was toxic - without even realizing it. The despair I felt that fateful morning in 2021 was the symptom of that toxicity, the same way that a stomach ache is a symptom of the poor choice of foods you made earlier that day. My life was a paradox, the tale of two opposite people, maybe even an oxymoron.

On the one hand, I still poured my heart and soul into people daily; family, friends, and coworkers would come to me for mentoring and advice. Envision a cup that you are constantly pouring out of. Now imagine that cup has dirt in it, some wads of paper, a golf ball maybe - how much less can that cup hold? That was me, so I kept clearing out all the debris in my cup. I forced myself to embrace a level of honesty I didn't think possible. Each week, I addressed another relationship, a new emotion and let go of another coping mechanism, and the golf balls, wads of paper, and dirt in my cup slowly began to dissipate.

Letting go of everything toxic in my cup was hard because I had never sat still in 2021 long enough to pinpoint the issue. How do you make sure you never fall down a deep dark hole if you don't know what the hole is? How do you protect yourself from something you don't know is dangerous? I felt like I was running without any clearly defined idea of what I was running from. I wasn't sure when I would be able to stop. I was afraid that I would always be chasing peace. At this point and time, I could define what I considered peace and knew I would know it when I found it. But I was afraid that the moment I stood still, despair would overtake me. I was tired of working, but I was more scared of despair. And so, I continued to work on myself. I continued to chase this image of peace I had in my mind and create a person who could embrace peace when it presented itself.

As the amount of healthy whole me, not toxic me that my cup could hold increased, the more of me people wanted. I thought I could just increase my capacity to meet demand, but that didn't work. I remember the overwhelming panic I had after realizing that even with all the work I had done and still was doing, I was slipping back into despair. I had to learn how to reserve enough of myself so I didn't feel empty. There is no manual for boundaries, and so it was all trial and error. I would allow others to make a statement, an event occur, or say "yes" when I thought "no" and feel the misalignment coming back into focus. I would have to backtrack, reset those expectations, and try again. I did a lot of apologizing, and that was draining. I was afraid others would think I didn't know my own mind and the reality was that I didn't. I was deathly afraid that setting boundaries in relationships would forever change them. I was afraid that when those I loved and cared about realized I was no longer the "go-to," their feelings for me would change. I was afraid that when I refused to be the "always-on" employee at work, opportunities for career growth would dwindle. Thankfully, I had those horrible memories from 2021 to fall back on, and my desire to leave those feelings behind was greater than my fear. Armed with that resolve, I slowly began to erect boundaries and, for the first time in my life, attempted to create and protect my peace.

Over fifty percent of the tears I have ever shed in my life were cried in 2022. I stopped wearing makeup for a while because I knew I would cry it off before the end of the day. Everyone talks about how great it feels to be authentic and live your truth, but not enough people talk about the painful work it takes to get there. Taking a hard look in the mirror every day, giving a name to the parts of you that needed to be stripped, and then slicing them away is hard. Most days, I felt like a surgeon performing an amputation on myself with no painkillers and only a butter knife. There was one day I spent crying because I had been a version of myself for others so long that I didn't even know what my original true self was or what I even wanted that to look like. I felt off balance most days, and that lack of surety in myself was something I had never experienced. It was strange because I knew so much of myself had to be cast aside, but I was dreading it at the same time. I found myself grieving for the familiar, even though I knew the familiar was toxic. I wanted desperately to let go of the beliefs and parts of my character that were no longer serving me, but I was scared at not knowing what would take its place.

As 2022 came to a close, I was one semester away from finishing my master's program. I had completed all the training to sit for my coaching examination through the International Coaching Federation (ICF). I had successfully graduated from both corporate development programs. I had even gotten to the place where I realized my house was no longer serving me and was actively looking for a new home. I did lose some friends throughout 2022, but I truly believe I'm better for it. Those relationships served their purpose, and I cherish the moments I shared with them, but there wasn't a place for them in the future that I was creating. The people in my life who truly love me and want the best for me have been nothing but encouraging and worked hard to see my point of view. Not all of them fully knew the amount of work I've done, and some of what I've written in this book may come as a surprise to them. But they loved me enough to say, "If this is important to you, then it's important to me."

SAUCERS OVER CUPS

In early 2023, I was introduced to a concept that I had never heard articulated but that I had apparently been chasing and living out the past two years. I was told that I needed to stop giving to others from my cup but rather from my saucer. I had to pour into others from my excess rather than taking what was meant for me - to keep me thriving, to keep me alive, to keep me functioning. That was a concept that I had never been exposed to, but that the work of the past year allowed me to accept and embrace with fervor.

What changed for me after that fateful morning in 2021 is that I can now define who I want to be and articulate expectations for myself. I no longer focus on making sure my cup is full. I make sure that it is overflowing so that I can serve others from my saucer. I've had to let go of the notion that focusing on "me" is selfish and instead focus on how much more effective I am when "me" is taken care of.

Throughout 2023, I told everyone that my goal was to "chase peace." I was adamant that if I didn't feel at peace, I would walk away and only press towards and chase after what embodied peace. Some may say that 2023 was the "important year" for me, but that couldn't be further from the truth. I would have never made it to 2023 without all the hard work that occurred in 2021 and 2022. Before 2023, I couldn't have defined peace for myself if my life depended on it. I couldn't have told you what I wanted and what good looked like for me. I was so focused on living for others that my feelings, emotions, and desires weren't formulated or acknowledged. Before all the work I did in 2022, I don't even think I could have accepted the idea of peace for myself. I had to let go of the familiar so peace could take place.

It's July 2023. The clock strikes six A.M., and my alarm is blaring. I jump out of bed with a smile on my face and peace in my heart. When I look out the window of my room, I see the bright colors of the tropical plants around the pool in Zimbabwe. I'm excited about the possibilities for the day and don't want a minute to go to waste. The coffee is already roasting, and I can't wait to meet my friend for sugar cane and a walk through her oasis. My mind was still. The only thoughts running through it were those I wanted to dwell on. And even those thoughts were wafting through rather than rushing recklessly. I was no longer running from the future or even hoping that an accident would keep me from having to deal with the future. Instead, I was running toward it with optimism, hope, and creativity. I could envision what good looked like for me and finally had the tools to create it. I had finally found peace.

ABOUT THE AUTHOR

Chenise Upshur is the CEO and founder of Cornerstone Coaching and Consulting, a company that focuses on developing and empowering leaders to better support their teams. Prior to this new and fast-growing venture, Chenise served as Chief of Staff for an SVP of North America sales in a top Fortune 500 company. It was her own personal journey of awareness and self-reflection that guided her on the path to following her passion of leader development.

During her near fifteen-year tenure in corporate America, Chenise has crafted an approach to leadership that centers on awareness and a desire to be a consummate learner of her craft. Chenise has won multiple accolades for her leadership skills and was recognized five times for having one of the top NPS scores globally as a leader.

Chenise also holds multiple degrees from Vanderbilt University and Lipscomb University, and is ICF accredited. Chenise is mom to an amazing middle schooler who is already almost a foot taller than she is. As the oldest of ten kids, family is important, and most weekends you can find her cheering someone on at a sporting event, attending after school activities, and hosting family brunch. Traveling is a big part of how Chenise learns new things whether it's across the world in another country or an hour drive away to check out a new museum, most long weekends and summer breaks are spent looking for new experiences.

https://www.cornerstonecoachingandconsulting.com/

4

ALAWNA RENEE OZOKA

REUNITE WITH YOUR POWER

To my loves, Ikemba and Somto. You are my inspiration to keep going.

∼

"There's no way it's already twelve p.m."

I shift my gaze from whatever document I have open on my laptop to the top right corner of my screen. I check again, and it is, in fact, twelve.

I was well-intentioned when I logged on in the morning. I told myself that I would take breaks to rest my eyes from the screen and get up from my desk to drink water and stretch my legs.

But no. It's already twelve.

And the only "break" I've had is finding a meme to accompany my "We made it to another day" message in the group chat.

Whatever five minute desk yoga video I had in my queue has been snoozed for the umpteenth time, and, come to think of it, I don't even remember taking a bathroom break.

A bit of guilt builds up in my chest as I blame myself for not following my plan to be more intentional with my day. Sadness about feeling guilty quickly follows. And, before I know it, I'm now mad that I'm sad that I feel guilty. It's an unforgiving cycle that continues until I eventually talk myself out of it and move on to the next thing. Does this sound familiar to you?

I wish I could say that what I've described is a one-off day for me, but I recall saying, "There's no way it's already twelve p.m." almost daily over the past couple of years.

LOW POWER MODE TURNED ON

This sort of time warp happened gradually before it became a staple in my routine. It began with the subtle infiltration of my morning routine. I *love* my mornings and have always been an early bird. For context, I was that person in college who was voluntarily up at eight in the morning, dressed and smiling in the front row of class. Under normal conditions, I reserve time to wake up mindfully before I get to work. I head downstairs and prepare my bowl of oatmeal and coffee—my very plain, but functional, bowl of oatmeal is complemented by my cup of coffee and sweet cremè creamer inside my *Root For Your Damn Self* mug. I prepare for my breakfast by opening up the blinds, allowing the sunshine to illuminate the dining room, and taking a few breaths for grounding. It's medicine for me to watch the day begin like this with feelings of safety and gratitude. After breakfast, I head back upstairs to take a hot shower complemented by some music, typically Lofi beats, or a Netflix rerun. And finally, before I even turn on my laptop, I read my devotional to prepare for any weapons trying to prosper in a direct message or email.

Morning after morning, I noticed my mindful breakfast by the window became shorter until it became eating at my work station. My sacred shower and self-care routine became rushed, too. Like *you only have hot water for five minutes so what are you going to do about it?* rushed. And my devotional time got pushed to later in the afternoon aka I didn't read it. All of these instances continued to add up until the math was not mathing for me.

One day, I found myself saying, "There's no way it's already twelve p.m." again. I had yet to take a break, and I was approaching an afternoon full of back-to-back meetings.

I remember calmly but firmly saying "Not today".

The funny thing about it is that nothing in particular happened that day. No one came at me incorrectly, nor was my schedule particularly unusual. In that moment, I just felt the magnitude of all the cherished moments taken from me, and I didn't feel like sharing them for another single second. I just checked myself on my truths:

Was I a hostage fastened to my chair? No.

Was I locked in a building without the key? No.

Was I stranded somewhere without transportation? No.

I was a whole human with free will, a car, and the power to click "Decline" on meeting invitations. So that's just what I did. I took time away from my physical work to support my soul-healing work. In the days proceeding, I continued to realize that I could give myself permission to do what worked best for me and my wellbeing.

The immediate results? Better sleep, reduced anxiety, and a pronounced resilience and peace in the presence of adversity. But the real impact was in how I saw myself: I finally got back to the real me and showed up in my power.

Collectively, I wonder how many time warp moments like these we can tally in our day that we're on autopilot. We become so caught up in the busyness of doing things that recalling what we did and why we did them becomes challenging.

If the research holds true and work continues to occupy one-third of our lives, there's an opportunity for more than thirty percent of our lives to be spent in movement without purpose. Now, I may not personally know you or your value system, but I'm going to speak up for both of us and say we wholeheartedly *reject* that projection.

Imagine what would be possible if we didn't wait for the weekend, retirement, or *insert occurrence here* to live more presently. The possibilities are endless of how much more fulfilling our lives could be if we toggled off autopilot and took back control of our trajectory! The encouraging truth is that living a present and purposeful life is very achievable, and it all starts with being aware.

THE NOD APPROACH

Between relationships, work, and all the other in-between responsibilities, I once thought that I didn't have the required time or knowledge to live mindfully. The idea of spending hours in meditation, backed by years of training and practice, seemed out of my reach. I thankfully learned a more present life does not require fancy training, an exhaustive routine, or the condition of fewer responsibilities. We begin to reclaim our power when we acknowledge what's happening around us and then decide how we want to respond to it, detailed further in what I call the NOD Approach.

Notice

Have you ever been so lost in thought while commuting that when you reach your destination, you have no idea how you got there, let alone arrived safely? I label this the "sleepwalking effect." It's when we go through the motions like eating, sleeping, and working without truly experiencing them. Taking moments to register our thoughts, feelings, physical sensations, and surrounding environment allows us to live with purpose. I've found that when I take time to really notice, my relationships grow deeper; my thoughts become clearer; and my resilience peaks in the face of adversity.

∼

Practice

Ten-second version: Narrate where you are

- Say aloud the date, time, and your physical location to ground yourself in the present moment.

Ten-minute version: Eat mindfully

- Start by reducing distractions and eating smaller portions to enhance the focus on your meal. Observe and savor the flavors, textures, and aromas of your food, eating slowly to fully experience each bite. Appreciate where it came from and the effort taken to prepare it. Reflect on the eating experience, noting the physical and emotional effects of your meal.

Observe

How many of us have heard or used the phrase "I'm feeling some type of way"? Welp, I'm here to announce that it's retired. We as humans are too valuable to dismiss or speak ambiguously about our experience. Instead, we will articulate specifically what we're feeling mentally, physically, and emotionally through observation.

The most important part of observation is doing so without judgment. As someone who finds comfort in labeling to protect myself, I get how challenging this part can be, so work with me a little here: when we name how we're feeling without qualifying or condemning it, we reclaim our control from negative self-talk, suppression of feelings, and emotional overwhelm. We can work towards addressing the root of what we need when we lay it all out there.

Practice

Ten-second version: Share a current feeling

- Write down at least one physical and emotional feeling (Bonus: Search 'The Feelings Wheel' to assist you in naming your specific feelings. I have it in the favorites section of my photos for easy access.)

Ten-minute version: Reflect on the present moment

- Find a quiet space and focus on deep breathing to ground yourself. Observe any emotions that surface without judging them, simply acknowledging their presence. Name any physical sensations felt in your body, avoiding the urge to analyze or categorize your feelings towards them. Whenever distracted, gently return your focus to your breath to maintain presence and awareness.

Decide

This is where we put it all together. Now that we understand what and how we're feeling, we can decide what we want to do about it. This is so simple yet so profound to me! Have you ever found yourself so caught up in routine that you overlooked your choice? Your ability to decide what you need to restore your sense of enough? Big hand raise for me! Sometimes we need to do something grand, like changing jobs or relocating. Other times we need to do something subtle, like eating lunch. And other times, we need to do nothing; yes, doing nothing is very much an active choice. The point is to fully and wholeheartedly do what makes it enough for you.

Practice

Ten-second version: Get a quick win

- Identify an action you can take right now to move you closer to enough.

Ten-minute version: Use the NOD Approach

- Use the tools we've discussed above to put Notice, Observe, and Decide in practice based on a recent event.

Self-Paced Guided Awareness Exercise

Notice*:* Become aware of how you are reading the book. Are you holding a physical copy or listening to an audio version? Focus your attention on your current location, whether you're reading or listening, and take note of the people and objects around you. Notice how your body is positioned without trying to manipulate your posture. Take inventory of anything else around you.

Observe*:* Bring your attention to how you are feeling physically and mentally. How do you feel about the way your body is positioned? If you perform a brief body scan from head to toe, what physical sensations can you name? Where do you feel relaxed, and where do you feel tension? Moving on to your mental state, what emotions are you feeling? Are you happy or sad? Content or dissatisfied? Energized or tired? Take note of all the mental and physical feelings you are currently experiencing.

Decide*:* To conclude, bring your attention to what you want to do with your mental and physical noticings and subsequent observations. Think about the allowances you can give yourself to make this moment enough for you. Remember, it's your world, I'm just the author reminding you of it! Perhaps there's a physical adjustment you want to make, like repositioning your seating or taking a couple of deep breaths. Maybe you want to eat or drink something. And maybe you've decided that you want to do nothing– which is very much still a decision. Give yourself permission to do what you need for you, and control what you can.

You can use this exercise as one of many resources to return your awareness to the present and enact meaningful change. The importance lies in giving yourself the grace to come back to your awareness without judgment.

BATTERY SUFFICIENTLY CHARGED

If you want a shortcut to being more in the moment, having a baby will get you there. As a new mom, I can money-back guarantee that. Becoming a mom to my son, Ikemba, has been the biggest blessing in waking me up; pun unintended, but for real, what is rest? I start each day with a strong sense of purpose, feeling entrusted with the responsibility to nurture and sustain life in this world.

These days, my morning routine starts off with him calling my name from the room next door and smiling from ear to ear when I walk in to pick him up. My breakfast now involves nursery rhymes and the little one sneaking spoonfuls of oatmeal he knows he doesn't like that eventually ends up on his bib. It also involves us spending a little extra time at the windows by the dining table to see the sunshine and, of course, play with the blinds. We continue our day with these moment-by-moment check-ins of what is enough for us.

Recently I found myself thinking, "There's no way it's twelve p.m.", but with a different lens.

I noticed that it was twelve, and my son was all too ready to hang out with his "muh-ma-ma", his words, not mine. We were both in the living room, me, lying down on my side and him sitting upright. We were on a plush purple blanket scattered with toys of all kinds. There were numbered blocks with vibrant colors to my left, a stacking ring set to my right, and a buzzing, singing, lightshow contraption in front of me.

After a while, I noticed my stomach start to make all these kinds of beatboxing noises. I recalled that it had been several hours since I had my breakfast. I also felt very restless. I had been sitting and engaging with the toys for so long that I felt confident I could recite each song playing from them word-for-word if a gameshow host asked me to.

I took a deep breath and decided that it was time for us to get up and get outside. And not in an angry "If we don't get the (word of choice) out of this house," but it was getting close to that. I laced up my shoes, put on my jacket, and grabbed my purse after securing my son in his car seat. Moments later, we were cruising down the road with 'Apples and Bananas' playing on the speakers—if you know, you know—on our way to get "muh-ma-ma" a delicious chicken wrap with Old Bay seasoned fries—again, if you know, you know.

In that moment, I kid you not, the combination of a deep breath and a chicken wrap truly saved my sanity. My whole day was in jeopardy of being a victim of the sleepwalker effect, where I just went through the motions and felt a sense of emptiness at night. Taking those few moments to check in with myself to be aware of my mood and surroundings turned my day into a joyful one, where I was able to be more present for my son and enough for myself.

Right now, it's X o'clock where you are, and I get it.

You've been in back-to-back meetings all day.

You've been caring for your children since early this morning.

You had to pick up an unexpected shift at work.

You've been driving rideshare since before the sun rose.

You've been supporting your aging loved ones.

"There's no way it's X o'clock", but it is.

Whether you're starting your day and want to set an intention of awareness, or you're ending your day and want to conclude on a more present note, I'm here to remind you that you have the power to change your current situation. You can give yourself permission to craft your outcome.

Notice where you're at.

Get curious about your observations without judgment.

Decide what to do next to make it enough for you.

And do it.

ABOUT THE AUTHOR

Alawna Renee Ozoka is a Certified Professional Life and Leadership Coach, Speaker, and 3X Founder. Her entrepreneurial journey began when she co-founded In Common, a platform to increase the economic wellness of the Black community. She later founded KIT (Keeping It Together) Strategies, an operations management consultancy that supports SMBs with their customer strategy.

While she is an operations and project management professional by trade, Alawna's passion is rooted in serving others. As an Authenticity & Alignment Coach, she partners with individuals looking to reunite with their inner power and own their voice. Alawna also serves as a speaker, leading inclusion talks around topics like owning uniqueness, pushing through fear, and living in purpose.

Whether it be coaching clients, collaborating with businesses, or speaking, Alawna's love for humanity fuels her next steps. It is her mission to expand access to systemically oppressed groups and amplify their voices.

https://www.alawnaozoka.com/

5

TIFFANY JOY MURCHISON

SETTING BOUNDARIES AND MINDING YOUR OWN BUSINESS

Picture this. Brooklyn. October 2000. 24-year-old me living in an affordable high-rise apartment in a decent neighborhood and driving a new but modest car. I was in my first year as a management employee at a Fortune 100 company, making more money annually than most of my elders had ever made. There was a strike that year, and managers had to work 12-hour days, seven days a week. But it did not bother me one bit. As a union employee, I learned from the old-timers to make the money when overtime was available. I carried that same philosophy with me into my management role and made close to six figures that year. So why the hell was I living paycheck to paycheck? Well, because I didn't know how to set boundaries and mind my own business.

What does not setting boundaries and not minding your own business look like? For me, it meant taking phone calls in the middle of the night with family drama, making Christmas happen for other people's children, and paying bills in homes that I didn't live in, to name a few. Before talking about how I learned to set boundaries and mind my own business, let me tell you how I got to the point of desperately needing to. My childhood was something like a dichotomy. My parents were 20 years apart, and their upbringing was as far apart as their age...

My father came from a locally prominent family in the Jim Crow South. My grandparents owned most of the businesses that served "colored" people in the 1930s and 40s in the tiny town of Badin, North Carolina. A brilliant man, my dad joined the Army and became a member of the Triple Nickles, the 555th Parachute Infantry Battalion, the nation's first All-Black parachute infantry test platoon, company, and battalion. In that little town of Badin he became known as a military "muckety-muck." After retiring from service, my father started several businesses, some successful and some not, helped start a newspaper, and was one of the first Black owners of a North Carolina automobile dealership. In 1979, my Dad founded the 555th Parachute Infantry Association, Inc., and was the organization's president from as far back as I can remember until his passing in 2021.

My mother's upbringing was completely different. She is a city girl, born and raised in Harlem, NY, by a family of mostly women who migrated from the French Quarters of New Orleans. Having always excelled in school, my mother graduated at the top of her class in high school with a diploma and a license in cosmetology. Her parents, however, believed in working a "good job" until you hit retirement age and then nothing but family gatherings and sleeping in. Couple that with an influential grandmother who thought my mother was beautiful enough to be a kept housewife. No matter how much the school counselor urged my mother to pursue higher education, there was no talk of college once the bell rang that signaled the end of the school day.

Nonetheless, she has always had visions of grandeur for as long as I can remember. It must have been difficult for my mother to be a little girl with big dreams raised by young parents who didn't seem to have many dreams of their own. My mother's big dreams were one of the reasons my parents got together. "He promised to put my name in lights," my mother said, "and he did." Together, my parents opened Sharon's Port, a bar located on the north shore of Long Island in Port Washington.

While they were from two different worlds, one thing my parents had in common was their expectation of me to be everything I could be and everything they weren't. Shortly after I was born—my mother's only child and my father's eighth (yes, I said eighth–of eleven!)—my parents bought a house in the suburbs. My childhood was filled with swing sets, Girl Scout Troops, Barbie Dream Houses, and every extracurricular activity in between. Education was a priority, and excellent grades were a must. From as early as I can remember, my mother would keep me up late into the night doing homework and perfecting school projects. "A little extra effort goes a very long way," she would say when I complained that I was tired and the work was "good enough." (I still hear her voice whenever I consider not giving something my all.) Dad's expectations played out more directly. Whenever I brought home a test with a less-than-perfect score, he would say, "Next time, it will be one hundred." My mother, however, always praised the 98 percent scores, too.

In the eyes of my maternal family, I was spoiled and born with a silver spoon in my mouth. Being what society deemed very pretty (especially for a little Black girl), brown-skinned with long curly hair past the middle of my back, I landed a few modeling jobs as a toddler. I lived in a middle-class suburb that was very diverse, especially for the time. I had white friends and friends from the Caribbean and Africa. My mother had a car, a red Monte Carlo, and my father "lived in our house" kind of. Those were things that back then, unbeknownst to me, were a sign that we "had money." Or at least we looked like we did. My perceived perfect childhood, juxtaposed with that of family members of the same generation, fostered a deep resentment that grew as we did.

The Southern "royal family of Badin," with matriarch Leila at the helm from North Carolina and sister Hattie enforcing from the North, had very different thoughts about my childhood; hell, about my very existence. The Murchison clan, and any extension thereof, had an etiquette to abide by and an image to uphold. My few memories of Grandma Leila are fond, but I can only recall seeing her in person on three occasions. I can't say the same for earlier memories of my interactions with the rest of my kinfolk. My father could do no wrong in either Leila's or Hattie's eyes, and his missteps quickly became the fault of any other party involved. For my siblings, who were just a couple of years younger than my mother and had children around my age, my mother and father's relationship went against the Murchison etiquette and image. Thus, so did my existence. Insert resentment.

Back to the dichotomy - too good for one side of the family, not good enough for the other, not accepted anywhere, not safe anywhere except alone in my room with my Barbie Dream House. When my cousins would come over, under the auspices of playing, there was bullying - like holding me down in the recliner, rocking it as hard as possible, and telling me I wasn't wanted here anymore, so I was being "rocked up to heaven." Where were the laws against shaken baby syndrome then? Visiting my family down south meant not being introduced to anyone at the church picnic because no one wanted to explain how my father had a daughter the same age as his grandchildren. However, I checked all the boxes for my parents - pretty, intelligent, well-behaved. I don't know why that wasn't enough. But the trauma of unacceptance left me feeling the need to prove two things: No, I don't think I am better than, and yes, I am good enough.

Insert learned behavior. Another thing my parents had in common was having a savior complex or white knight syndrome - the need to "save" people by fixing their problems. Especially when they were together, but even after they split, my parents were the go-to for folks with all sorts of problems, money usually being at the top of the list with a place to live a very close second. Once they could no longer physically or financially continue their knight-in-shining-armor behavior, they both heaped their self-inflicted responsibilities on me.

My mother carried the guilt of changing her circumstances, and with that came the belief that she was *supposed* to *be there* for her family, no matter what. It was "the right thing to do." She made excessive personal sacrifices and forced those sacrifices on me. She would give away my things, often under the auspices of "loaning," and tell me I was selfish if I protested. "They are less fortunate than you," she would say to which I screamed, under my breath," That's not my fault!" Who *borrows* a cabbage patch doll anyway? I never saw Margot again. By the time I was a teenager, I felt smothered under the weight of my mother's need to save the world. All the while, she was burning herself out and sacrificing me.

I believe my father's savior complex was born out of unresolved trauma in his past coupled with the expectations of his parents. My father always thought his way was right and that he had the solution to everyone else's problems and how they could improve their lives if they just followed his instructions. Some of that attitude could be attributed to the fact that people were always asking him for money. He used to say, "If you don't want my advice, don't ask for my money." I can't say that I disagree with that, though.

While there was always something in me that was uncomfortable, resentful even, about "helping" those less fortunate than me, I absolutely played the savior role longer than I have not. I also made excessive personal sacrifices, putting others' needs before mine. My rationale was that I had a good job and knew where my next paycheck would come from, but they didn't. (That's a story for another book.) I paid other people's rent before paying my own, played the "rich auntie," and didn't take my dream vacations or buy things I wanted because, God forbid, someone would need the money I'd just spent going to the Bahamas. And the more I gave, the more people expected. And, oh, the fallout, if I'd dare say no—a family discussion that pointed out how I'd always been spoiled and selfish that left me riddled with guilt.

REVELATION

One day, a day when I was absolutely mentally, emotionally, physically, and financially drained, I called my favorite aunt for a listening ear and a bit of wisdom. At some point during the conversation, trying to make sense of my circumstances, I told her, "God never gives you anything you can't bear." Without hesitation, she rebutted, "Did God give you all of that stuff, or did you just pick it up on your own? Go ask Him."

Just as we often lean on that adage about God never giving us more than we can bear, people of all walks of life also lean on another biblical tenant that says we can do all things with God. My aunt's question challenged me to take a deeper look at the scripture that is rooted in Philippians, chapter four, verse 13, normally recited as "I can do all things through Christ who strengthens me." But when I looked at another version, the Amplified, it reads, "I can do all things [which He has called me to do] through Him who strengthens and empowers me [to fulfill His purpose..." Wait. What? *Which He has called me to do?* I felt like someone turned on all the lights. Immediately, I could hear God say, "Fool, I did not tell you to do all of those things!"

That scripture, those words as simple as they may seem, brought on the awareness that was the catalyst for me to set boundaries and mind my own business. I began diving deeper into scripture, looking for more clarification. I continued to find evidence that people should be helping themselves more than I was, like the Parable of the Talents in Matthew Chapter 25. Various sermons about self-preservation that I'd previously glossed over as not pertaining to me now started to resonate. I got a great therapist and started to unpack the dichotomy and resentment, leading to a greater understanding of what my assignments [from God] were and what they were not.

TWO KEY ELEMENTS TO SETTING BOUNDARIES

Remember that episode of Bugs Bunny where Bugs dares Yosemite Sam to step over this line, and Yosemite steps over without hesitation? The dance continues, with Bugs daring Yosemite, "This one, that one, that one, this one," until eventually, Yosemite Sam steps one too many times and falls off the cliff. Well, that's what it's like in real life when you try setting boundaries for someone else, except it's you who falls off the proverbial cliff. Setting boundaries is not about telling someone what they better not do or what you will not tolerate but rather about one, the *behavior* you exhibit that clearly articulates what you will and won't tolerate and two, your response when someone crosses those boundaries with actions that are uncomfortable, disrespectful, or harmful to you. The most crucial element of setting boundaries is that they are for you.

The second most crucial element of setting a boundary is the consequence. The lack of consequences is why we witness behaviors escalate, and situations worsen. For example, a boy who manhandles his high school sweetheart without punishment will most likely grow up to be a husband who abuses his wife and maybe even his children. A family member who repeatedly borrows money with a promise to pay it back and doesn't will continue to do so as long as you continue to lend. No consequence. No change. My Pastor, Dr. AR Bernard, says it best. People don't change until the pain of staying the same is greater than the pain of change. A boundary without a consequence is simply a wish. And no one likes when wishes don't come true.

WHAT I LEARNED ABOUT THE BENEFITS OF SETTING BOUNDARIES

When I started setting boundaries for myself, whoa! The freedom! It's like a drug. You set and stick to one boundary, and the next thing you know, you're a boundary-setting superstar. Here's what I learned:

Setting boundaries prevents future conflict. While it's not exactly healthy to cut folks off immediately at the first sign of something we aren't fond of (unless they're giving off abuser or serial killer vibes), setting boundaries at the onset of any relationship is essential. Like my great-grandmother used to say, "start out how you can hold out." If you aren't comfortable with a behavior initially, don't glance over it for fear of losing the relationship. It will not get better.

Setting boundaries empowers you and builds greater self-esteem. Respecting yourself enough to command respect from others does wonders for your self-worth and leads to healthy self-preservation.

Setting boundaries develops independence. We often don't enforce boundaries because we don't want to lose the relationship with that person, but we then lose our relationship with ourselves. Setting boundaries frees you from the feeling that you need "them," no matter how toxic they may be. When you realize that the boundary didn't kill you or them, you let go of the trauma bond and move on.

Hand in hand with developing independence, setting boundaries decreases the occurrence of toxic behaviors and relationships and allows you to focus on your emotional and mental health. Let's be clear, toxicity is not an "it's not me, it's them" situation. It takes two to tango, and not having boundaries IS toxic behavior. However, as you move away from toxic relationships, it's almost impossible not to focus on your own mental and emotional well-being because now you have space for healing to begin

Setting boundaries also minimizes burnout because you will no longer commit yourself to people and things that you don't actually have the capacity to manage. You and the folks around you will have more respect for your time, talent, and treasury.

MINDING YOUR OWN BUSINESS

The phrase minding your own business is a double entendre, and both meanings are equally essential to a fulfilling life. Let's start with the most common meaning - staying out of other people's affairs. There's more to that thought than just not being a busybody. As I said earlier, when you are born into the savior complex role, the guilt that comes with your [perceived] success leads to taking on a lot of responsibility. No, scratch that. Burden. That's what it is— other people's burdens. The secondary meaning of the phrase minding your own business leans on the definition of [to] mind, meaning to take care of someone or something, to regard [it] as important, or to feel concerned about [it]. In other words, mind or tend to your own business, affairs, and life.

After having been freed by the Amplified version of Philippians 4:13, I approach every decision to get involved with the question, "Is this my assignment?" Whether helping someone or taking on a new client, it always boils down to that same question. Is this my assignment? The peace that came with setting boundaries has provided a formula to answer that question. If I feel at peace about getting involved, it most likely is a [God-given] assignment, and when my spirit feels unsettled, it's most certainly not.

WHAT I LEARNED ABOUT MINDING MY OWN BUSINESS

Minding your own business saves time and makes more money. Have you ever really thought about how much time you spend on other people's business? Here's a quick story. One afternoon, I received a phone call from a few relatives all up in arms about a situation that none of us could do a darn thing about. It should have been my cue to exit stage left when the "he said, she said, they said" narrative started. Instead, I tried to offer a different perspective, which made them pissed at me. Before I knew it, I had been conversing for 45 minutes about something that had nothing to do with me. I thought of all the income-generating things I could have done and promised never to waste time like that again

Minding your own business gives you more control. The less you have on your plate, the better you can manage the tasks at hand and crush your goals. Remember, only clowns work hard to juggle 12 balls simultaneously.

Minding your own business increases your impact. When you are not spread too thin with tasks that are not your assignment, you have a more significant positive impact on the things you are assigned to do. Whether it's having more time to spend with your loved ones, perfecting a new workshop you're developing, or heading to the gym, the gift of your presence at greater lengths increases the benefit.

Minding your own business presents more learning opportunities by making room in your conscious and subconscious for new ideas and information. Not only will you have more time to be a lifelong learner, but you will also find that you can consume and retain information more easily.

Minding your own business makes you better equipped to help others when it is actually your assignment or responsibility to do so. For example, tending to the business in my own household allowed me to prepare better to provide my children with a college education or support my parents in their senior years.

STEPS TO SETTING HEALTHY BOUNDARIES AND MINDING YOUR OWN BUSINESS

Understand that your new boundaries and attention to your own business will be just as uncomfortable for the people around you as they are for you. You have to commit to the process. The people around you are comfortable, and your behavior will reveal their true character. Some of it will be ugly. People who love you will eventually applaud and get in line. People who only lust for what you do for them will exit. And your first lesson is that their departure is not your business.

- Get a new hobby. You will find that your phone will ring less, and you will have free time in your hands when you set boundaries and mind your own business. This new lifestyle can start to feel lonely and it will be tempting to fall back into old habits. So, find something else positive to do. I began by volunteering at my church. It allowed me to still help people, but without using money. And now, I'm learning to play golf. Whatever you choose to do, know that while you were saving others, you were killing parts of you. Time to give you life more abundantly.
- Take inventory of your boundaries or lack thereof. Do you say yes to everything? Do you put others before yourself?

Write down ways you can add balance to your life by developing boundaries.
- Take an honest inventory of your feelings in circumstances where boundaries are needed. How do you respond when you feel disrespected? If your response is unhealthy, set boundaries regarding how you will and will not respond.
- Write this down 100 times or until you never forget it. "No" is a complete sentence. You don't need to explain why you will not or can not; doing so diminishes your authority.
- Communicate your expectations and, when necessary, use your words. Setting boundaries is more about action—adhering to how you've decided to respond—than words. Nonverbal communication works wonders.
- Use technology to your advantage. Put your phone on Do Not Disturb so that you can get a good night's rest without interruptions from everyone with a problem in the middle of the night. Let calls go to voicemail. Especially the calls from messy people. You have heard their nonsense a million times, and frankly, it's not your business.
- Don't give the responsibility to someone else—take accountability. You cannot expect someone else to honor your boundaries when you don't, so take accountability for your role, especially if you simply have wishes. The great thing about taking accountability is that it comes with the authority to make the changes necessary for better future outcomes.
- Turn the tables. I chuckle as I think about another aunt's advice. When you get a phone call from someone who usually calls to dump their problems on you and ask for money, start telling them what bills you have due and all the errands you could use help with before they can even get the words out. Watch how fast they get off the phone and peep the technique. "Well, let me go, I need to…" Add that line to your arsenal.

- Stop being nosey and mind your business. Do not dive deeper into people's problems. Asking questions signals that you want to help solve the problem.

NOW, GO TAKE THE TRIP TO THE BAHAMAS!

I hope that this snippet into my life has equipped you with enough information to begin your journey of discovery. Setting boundaries and minding your own business is absolutely challenging, but it is necessary for a life full of joy and peace. Not setting boundaries and not minding your own business allows negativity to creep into almost every area of your life. Well, positivity cannot exist where negativity is allowed to roam free. Remember that you are responsible for your own happiness and success. Set boundaries, mind your own business, and live the life you were truly meant to live. Take that trip to the Bahamas! You have the power. Own it. Embrace it! I certainly have.

ABOUT THE AUTHOR

Tiffany Joy Murchison is a consummate communications professional and an influential entrepreneur leading a Brooklyn, NY-based boutique public relations firm. As the founder and principal public relations strategist for TJM & Co. Media Boutique, Tiffany Joy leads a team to empower brands to flourish by exposing them to ideal audiences through fully integrated, purpose-focused public relations and digital marketing strategies.

Tiffany Joy's professional experience spans several industries, from communications, technology, and financial services to publishing and entertainment. She also has over 20 years of experience in nonprofit board management. In 2019, TJ published her first e-book, *PRY Until...* The small business owner's guide to DIY public relations until you're ready to hire a pro. A second edition, which discusses managing reputation during social unrest and a health pandemic, was published in 2020.

Tiffany Joy is a Goldman Sachs 10k Small Business Program graduate and holds a Bachelor's in Public Administration and Communications from The City College of New York. Her most notable certifications include a Project Management Certificate from Villanova University, Business Certificates in Entrepreneurship from Cornell University and Babson College, and a certification in DEI Communication Strategies from PRSA. Recognized as one of Crain's New York 2023 Notable Leaders in Marketing, Advertising, and PR, Tiffany Joy believes in serving the community and embodies her company's tagline, "Where PR meets purpose." She is actively involved in various organizations, including serving on the Brooklyn Chamber of Commerce Board of Directors and several Chamber committees. Tiffany Joy is a Digital Girl, Inc. board member, leading their PR and fundraising committee. Moreover, she mentors Black and women entrepreneurs through programs with NYC Small Business Services. In 2024, Tiffany Joy joined the executive board of the Black Public Relations Society as Vice President and Chair of Professional Development Programs. Her favorite role, however, is being a mom. Tiffany and her family currently live in Brooklyn, NY.

6

KAYLEIGH O'KEEFE

EXCELLENCE IN AWARENESS

YOUR ENERGY SPEAKS

My boss, the CEO of a fast-growth technology start-up, said to me one morning, "Kayleigh, I know whether this entire company is going to have a good day or a bad day based on how you walk through the door." And let me tell you, on this particular day, he did *not* mean this as a compliment. I had ripped through the front door like a tornado, in a huff and a frenzy, already feeling slighted by the torrent of emails from our key client in my inbox. The entire company, I suppose, was in for a day of 90 mph whiplash, given my mood.

Until that moment, I had thought that it was generally a good thing that I couldn't keep a poker face or hide my feelings. Didn't my transparency help signal to the outside world what was going on within? Perhaps, but it sure isn't helpful if your signal is set to one radio station of anxiety, stress, and negativity. I was drowning in fear that I was not good enough or experienced enough to build and lead our new customer success team, and this fear emanated a torrent of unease into my environment. I didn't know what to do with my CEO's comment except to self-flagellate and limp around like a wounded puppy.

It would take me many years to fully understand the lesson encoded in this 10-second interaction, simple as it was: Your energy is everything. It comes from your emotion, and your emotion comes from feelings, and behind feelings is the source of everything…your belief system. So many of us are walking around with belief systems that were *introjected* into us from ages zero to six through our family, culture, religion, and so on that have gone completely unexamined and unquestioned. The vast majority of humans live their lives based on assumptions (beliefs) that lock in a certain range of emotions. This emotional range is very, very limited and many humans are playing the same playlist of fear, guilt, and shame—with one song of joy or gratitude shuffled into the mix sporadically and infrequently. Behind this tiny spectrum of emotion are a series of unexamined beliefs running the entire show subconsciously. These beliefs are so ingrained that they are hard to spot.

Two of the beliefs that were running my show when my CEO commented on my negative energy were:

1. I must suffer until no one else suffers, a common belief held by naturally empathic people who grew up in narcissistic homes or were raised in Christianity (both are true for me), and
2. I can't be happy or proud until I accomplish the goal, meaning it "must be hard," and I can only express joy if I succeed, not while I am in the process of pursuing the goal.

Of course, I didn't realize these beliefs were running my program at the time, but over the last ten years, I've been called to experiences, teachers, and tools that have helped me cultivate a deep sense of inner awareness and inspired me to live with "Excellence in Awareness" as my primary way of being. Mastering one's mind, body, and soul so that it is a channel for limitless creation is the opportunity of our time, but it is only available to us if we walk the path of self-awareness, which starts with suspending everything we thought we knew.

SUSPEND YOUR BELIEFS

Thankfully, awareness is putting many people on right now. Since 2020, there has been an acceleration of global awakening as more individuals are beginning to pause long enough to question their beliefs and open themselves up to higher states of consciousness and evolution. In my work as the founder of Soul Excellence Publishing, I have witnessed and supported over 500 individuals from sixteen countries to write about their experiences of awakening to deeper truths about who they really are. These individuals-turned-authors have each revealed the moments that shook them awake and the choice they had to either power through and continue on with life as usual or to step back, reconsider their values and way of living, and consciously choose to take responsibility for a new way of being. It takes tremendous inner strength to live in alignment with one's values in a world programming us daily to conform to one version of reality. The stories I publish, like the chapters you are reading in this very book, are meant to reveal how people are navigating pain, loss, and defeat (sometimes self-inflicted) and choosing to reclaim their inner power as creative beings. It is not easy work, but it is essential in these modern times.

In the rest of my chapter, I want to share with you how I continue to pursue "Excellence in Awareness" and live in deeper alignment with my personal values.

EXPAND YOUR SENSE OF SELF

We are living at a time when we are being bombarded with messages to attach to a limited sense of identity. We are being told to construct - and reinforce - our sense of self based on skin color, sexuality, nationality, religion, politics, and so on. We are encouraged to take tremendous pride in these things and to form associations based on these traits, some immutable and some chosen. Over-identifying with any of these things limits our power as creative beings because it locks us into a set of beliefs (again, often from childhood and often gone completely unquestioned) that determine our actions. Remember, beliefs form feelings and motivate action, which create energy, and energy is our point of attraction. We are SO much more than these characteristics and these beliefs, and perhaps this is why this knowledge is not only kept from us, but also why these messages are constantly reinforced in our media landscape and societal discourse. A distracted person is an easy person to control. A fearful person is an easy person to control. A person with a strong set of unquestioned beliefs is an easy person to control. An aware, curious, calm person is a wildcard, and society does not like rebels!

What if your beliefs are actively keeping you from experiencing your full human power?

I know mine have.

WHAT THE TIME IS CALLING FOR

Now is not the time to take up arms, become an activist, or pledge allegiance to this group or that one. To do so in this particular moment of human evolution is to continue to give away your innate power and knowingness to an outside authority. You must, for this moment, overcome your desire to belong, which, if examined closely, is a fear-born desire of abandonment and ostracization, which each of us can relate to, and allow yourself to step into the void of the unknown and the possible. Isn't it interesting that so much of our media culture is about inclusion and belonging, but the tactics to bring about that goal feel, to me, at an energetic level, coercive and cult-like? How can we feel included and belong if we are not clear on who we really are - beneath the superficial externals and even the long-held beliefs? What are you sacrificing in terms of your values, interests, and ideals when you trade personal sovereignty for group cohesion? It's a worthy question in these times.

If now is not the time to seek safety in groups that still operate from fear, even if they proclaim a message of love, then what IS it a time for, exactly?

UNPLUG FROM THE MATRIX

Now *is* the time to set aside the never-ending stream of media pumping into your brain and further distancing yourself from your inner wisdom. How can you possibly know how you feel and what you think if you are in a rushing river of other people's opinions? It is not possible. I am quite guilty of this as someone who loves listening to podcasts to learn new things. However, I've noticed how easily I move from episode to episode, concept to concept, without giving myself proper time and space to sit with the ideas and run them through my own internal information filter and inner compass. I've had to become much more aware of this habit and take the time to:

1. Determine what question I am considering and search for a person or idea to listen to
2. Take notes during the episode on things that challenge me or stir me up in some way
3. Reflect on how what I am hearing is challenging my beliefs - and open myself up to change my beliefs and
4. Engage in real-life conversation with real humans, ideally face to face, on a particular subject.

We are at the dawn of a new era with artificial intelligence, and it will be easier than ever to be emotionally manipulated into straying far from your values if you are not careful.

What commitment can you make to connect to your inner wisdom?

SPEND TIME IN NATURE

Now *is* the time to consciously spend more time in nature. What secrets does the natural world have for us to discover if only we spend more time with her? My life has improved dramatically by taking the time each morning to walk to the intracoastal waterway near where I live and witness the sunrise. I feel my entire body turn on at a cellular level as the sun's rays hit my face. I say "good morning" to every red-headed woodpecker and flower I encounter on my walk, and I especially give thanks for any dolphins I happen to see playing in the water. Our collective nervous systems are completely out of whack at this moment, wired for fear, activated into fight or flight on the regular, and causing serious distortions in our awareness. Settling into nature by placing your feet on the ground or gazing far off into the horizon are natural, free remedies for calming the CNS and creating inner spaciousness for new awakenings and ah-has to drop into our core being.

How do you see yourself spending more unstructured time in nature?

TAKE PRISTINE CARE OF THE BODY

Now *is* the time to take pristine care of our bodies. Our bodies are the great tuning forks of the universe. Our bodies can be tuned to peace, joy, and abundance, or they can be tuned to fear, guilt, and shame. The choice is ours, but oftentimes, it doesn't feel like it is because we have let our bodies go and turn against us. Our biology is running our show, and it is so deeply connected to outdated beliefs and related feelings. While I have always been a spiritual seeker and have long been on the path of personal growth, expansion, empowerment, and, ultimately, liberation, so much of what I was studying and seeking to apply in my life could not break through the physical barrier of my body. What do I mean?

In simple terms, despite my dedication to my "inner work," the results of that work - and the true embodiment of the lessons - were kept at bay in my life until I decided to put down alcohol. Once I made the decision to treat my body like the earthly temple it is and stop poisoning myself with alcohol, the dam broke, and suddenly, my body was able to receive the wisdom on a deeper level and came back into complete restoration. There were many beliefs associated with alcohol that I had to become aware of and release back into the ether, beliefs like I don't belong, so I must drink to fit in; it's perfectly social and acceptable to have a drink now and again; I deserve champagne for all of my hard work, and so on. The body is the most powerful tool for awareness that we have, yet we are taught to distrust it.

What beliefs about your body and health are dictating how you treat yourself?

SHOCK YOURSELF, SHOCK THE WORLD

We are at a great moment of human awakening and consciousness. As you become more aware and decide to question your beliefs and choose something different that aligns with what you value and what feels good, you will shock the people in your life. Not everyone is going to heed the obvious calling that something is not quite right in our world and that the beliefs and assumptions we've operated under are not holding true. Your journey will require tremendous courage. Your relationships will change. Your work will transform. Your environment may need a total upgrade. Trust. Trust that when you are connected back to your heart, partially via my suggestions above regarding reducing your media consumption, spending time in nature, and taking care of your body, you will sense truth and fiction.

Perhaps the stories that you grew up with about your family, your heroes, your God, your nation, your entire world, in fact, are pure fiction. The virtues of truth, wisdom, discernment, discipline, beauty, and love are your very best companions in this moment of awakening. Not everyone will rise with you as you expand your awareness, but know that there are many of us, and you are reading our stories right in this very book, who are with you on this path.

AMPLIFYING THE WISDOM OF CONSCIOUS LEADERS

Years ago, when I started Soul Excellence Publishing, I wrote down my mission for the company: To amplify the wisdom of conscious, courageous leaders. At the time, I did not fully appreciate how prescient that mission was or even what those words really meant; they had just flown from my heart down to my fingers and onto the keyboard. They felt right and true even if I didn't know where they came from. From that simple statement, I have birthed universes, and each book that I've published has facilitated deep awakenings of the soul for both authors and readers.

I am a messenger. I am here to inspire others as I navigate the continual expansion of my own consciousness and deeper realization that I am a creator of entire universes, and so, my friend, are you. To create what we want, we must do massive inner clean-up, followed by regular spring cleanings, so that we are as clear channels as possible for our highest consciousness to flow through us. We are beings of light and frequency, reverberating with a signature that is created in each moment via our attention and awareness. To be unaware - whether by living in pessimistic fear or putting rose-colored glasses on - is to abdicate responsibility for creating the most honest and abundant life possible.

Your awareness *has* put you on. You are reading this book. Some things will click immediately; other lessons may require years of repeating the same lesson over and over again until you are finally willing to receive the wisdom and let go of suffering. Trust your journey in this lifetime, and if there is one belief I would suggest to you it is this one: *believe that you are an empowered individual capable of rewriting your story at any moment in time.*

ABOUT THE AUTHOR

Kayleigh O'Keefe is a USA Today bestselling author, speaker, and founder and CEO of Soul Excellence Publishing, the publishing house for Empath Leaders.

Sometimes referred to as a puppy for her endless energy, optimism, and playfulness, she is also quite serious about helping others reconnect to their soul, pursue excellence on their terms, and spark new cultural movements. Founded in 2020, Soul Excellence Publishing has published 17 international bestselling books featuring over 550 Empath Leaders from 16 countries across four continents.

Kayleigh received her bachelor's from Duke, an M.B.A. from the University of San Francisco, and has fifteen-plus years of experience advising Fortune 500 executives and building commercial teams at early-stage start-ups. She also hosts *The Future is Human* podcast, where she explores how to upgrade our human operating system so that we can experience deeper intimacy and connection. She leads by example, always allowing for her own expansion and seeking to master the inner game of life.

Kayleigh loves being an aunt and brings "aunt energy" to all of her endeavors, pushing the limits of what's possible and what's expected. She has walked over four hundred miles across two different routes of The Way of St. James pilgrimage through Spain and Portugal.

After spending most of her career in Washington, D.C. and San Francisco, she now lives by the beach in Hollywood, Florida, where she makes it a point to see the sunrise every morning, cultivate her yoga practice, practice tennis, and live by her values of inner harmony, being in nature, intimacy, vitality, and prosperity.

https://soulexcellence.com/

PART II

LEADERSHIP & PROFESSIONAL DEVELOPMENT

"If your actions create a legacy that inspires others to dream more, learn more, do more and become more, then, you are an excellent leader."

— DOLLY PARTON

7

SAMANTHA J. A. ARMSTRONG

JOURNEY TO AUTHENTICITY: NAVIGATING THE RHYTHM OF INNER TRUTH

SEARCHING FOR THE BEAT IN NO MAN'S LAND OF SELF-DISCOVERY

As a child, I was a dreamer and adventurer who wanted to experience the world limitlessly. White water rafting was a total rush, and I'd let my imagination run just as wild, daydreaming and wandering in books that took me to fictional worlds. My love of dance, with its focus on the physical, offered a unique expression of my quiet yet untamed spirit. Reading and writing was my sanctuary—a place where I could mold reality into the imaginary and breathe life into my dreams.

But my carefree spirit wasn't nurtured in the environment I grew up in; neither was the confidence to express what I wanted or even who I was.

My parents emigrated from Jamaica to the United States in their twenties, and both Jamaican and military cultures shaped my upbringing. My dad dedicated 24 years to the Air Force, so I spent most of my childhood around military bases across Europe. Balancing the conservative and traditional values of both cultures, I internalized the familiar belief that children should be seen and not heard. Despite wanting to question rules, structures, and tradition, I withheld my questions and opinions. As an introverted and introspective child, the blend of these influences, coupled with navigating my queer identity, presented a complex and isolating journey of self-discovery. Finding my voice was challenging.

As the child of immigrants and a first-generation college student, I felt the weight of expectations to excel academically and professionally. I vividly recall attempting to use whiteout, albeit unsuccessfully, to change a grade lower than an A on my middle school report card. This pursuit of perfection persisted into my career as I searched for external validation and the prestige associated with prominent companies and traditional career paths, even when they didn't align with my authentic self.

I wanted examples of someone navigating the nuanced, gray, in-between space—somewhere between gay and straight, between Jamaican and American, an introvert needing deep connection, and desiring both family and a career. It felt like a no man's land of self-discovery. How was I to know myself when there were no visible representations, and examples I saw didn't resonate with my soul?

LEARNING THE SYNCHRONIZED DANCE OF FAMILY & CAREER

Growing up I internalized a lot of ideas about marriage and career from witnessing adults navigating common challenges in a military environment. Seeing them struggle with issues such as deployments, infidelity, financial pressures, mental health, and gender roles led to my narrow assumptions about career and relationships.

Watching my mom and other women dedicate their lives to caring for their families left an impression on me. The military women my dad worked with were the career women I witnessed throughout my childhood. I'd see them in their uniforms, seemingly strong and independent, and struggled to see myself in them. The traditional dichotomy of femininity associated with a nurturing, stay-at-home mom and military spouse, and masculine energy aligned with a successful career felt limiting. I recognized my own demeanor as softer and what I perceived as feminine, yet I wanted *both* a fulfilling profession and a family. I knew I wanted more than the examples I saw. At work I've chased fancy titles at prestigious organizations and imitated more masculine behaviors, while at home I was resisting the instinct to nurture. It all felt unnatural, created distance in my relationships, and increased my mental load.

Now, with a broader perspective, I respect the diversity of paths people choose. For my mom, family was her top priority, a conscious choice I truly appreciate as an adult. I am grateful for people who dedicate themselves to caregiving, acknowledging the impact of their commitment. This ongoing process of unlearning and reframing has given me insight into and empathy for the different desires women have when navigating choices between family and career.

Throughout my career, I've since met remarkable women who painted the picture of what is possible as a working mom. These women each have a unique blend of strength, independence, and nurturing qualities. Their ability to succeed in the professional world with grace and resilience while also being empathetic challenged the narrow perspectives that I had internalized.

Witnessing other working parents, I've realized that my introverted and feminine qualities are not obstacles but gifts that I bring to my work. The dichotomy I once perceived began to blur as I saw women thriving personally and professionally, challenging societal norms that had influenced my early perspective and the way I showed up professionally. For example, I would shapeshift and try to act as a high-energy extrovert, suppressing my introverted nature, all driven by fear of deviating from workplace norms and avoiding potential biases or discrimination.

Inspired by other women, I've since learned that one can be assertive and nurturing, ambitious in one's career, and devoted to one's family. Authenticity in the form of embracing both my introspective nature and my ambitious aspirations is not only possible, but crucial for fulfillment and impact. This revelation unfolded when I participated in a six-week group coaching program centered on the divine feminine. Starting the program with uncertainty, I left with a greater understanding of how to genuinely embrace my feminine power, as well as a clearer grasp of what authentic expression of the masculine looks like for me.

STUMBLING THROUGH DISJOINTED CHOREOGRAPHY

Cultivating a meaningful career was critical to my sense of fulfillment, yet the struggle to be authentic and vulnerable kept me from articulating my needs. It was a gradual process to outgrow the influence of my upbringing on my confidence—to learn to trust my instincts, articulate my needs, and embrace my power.

To this day, the words of a former boss stick with me.

"You seem overwhelmed," he said during a one-on-one meeting. And he was right; juggling administrative burdens and lack of resources hindered me from doing meaningful work. I shared my concerns that the situation was not conducive to success.

His response shocked me: "I completely understand if you're not focused on your career now, if you'd rather be at home with your child. I wouldn't fault you for it if you don't want to be here."

But I hadn't mentioned my child in our conversation. I was intentional about keeping my son off-camera while working remotely, trying to manage the complexities of a demanding work-life balance. On one hand, his words triggered a response within me. Inferring that I should be a stay-at-home mom brought back naïve childhood impressions of unfulfilling sacrifice – a place I had avoided. On the other hand, it confirmed that my dedication to work was being questioned since becoming a parent.

Even before joining this team, my instinct was that the team culture and leadership weren't aligned with my needs. On paper it seemed like a dream job, but during the interview process, I sensed tension in the team dynamics.

Nevertheless, I accepted the job. Falling back into an old habit, I was selling myself a dream instead of confronting the reality before me. I romanticized situations and bypassed the clear red flags in front of me. This time was no different.

On the other side of the hiring process, the toxicity I suspected was confirmed, evolving into a challenging chapter in my career. The lack of trust between my boss and me confirmed my initial concerns. Despite doing my job, establishing critical client relationships, and ticking all the boxes, my boss scrutinized my work behind my back, casting doubt at every turn.

My upbringing instilled in me a complacency with "good enough," a mindset I generally embraced—until that moment, and his comment forced me to listen to my body. Our bodies inherently know what's right for us; we feel it. Sometimes, articulating that intuition is challenging, and when it's hard to articulate, it's scary to follow it.

In that pivotal moment, the realization struck me—it was time to leave. Although I had acknowledged the dysfunction many times before, those words marked the tipping point. The need for change was undeniable, a choice I had to make for my own well-being.

My heart pounding and stomach in a knot, I unapologetically confronted my boss about the inappropriate mention of my son in that conversation. As expected, he dismissed it, treating it as trivial. Speaking up directly in that moment was liberating, even with the foresight that the outcome wouldn't be positive. The discomfort wasn't as overwhelming as expected, and it became another clear confirmation that it was time to go.

Shortly after, I left the company. Without a job secured and uncertain about what was next, I felt liberated by leaning fully into my faith. The decision made me feel empowered, recognizing my agency over both my career and life. I was confident that the relationships and reputation I had built would guide me intentionally in my next career move.

That confidence was partially because this wasn't my first time in this situation; I'd lived this same scene before, knowingly walking into a bad situation that I'd ultimately have to leave. It felt like a recurring pattern, akin to navigating a tumultuous relationship with corporate America. Despite my initial belief that this organization was more evolved than it proved to be, it, like so many others, cultivated an environment that wasn't built for people of color. A lack of representation in leadership, coupled with hollow DEI initiatives and a lack of sponsors working towards equitable systems, highlighted the systemic challenges faced by underrepresented minorities.

I realize that in this work environment and related situations, I wasn't building resilience by pushing through what wasn't meant for me; I was merely surviving. The cycle of ruminating and replaying trauma in my mind had wired my brain to operate from a place of fear. I was living in a perpetual state of fight, flight, or freeze. Masking my truth to fit a mold and trying to please those around me, whether it was my parents, my boss, or my partner, became a pervasive pattern in my life.

Research shows that people with a history of trauma often wrestle with challenges related to authenticity and vulnerability.[1] People from marginalized groups tend to face higher instances of trauma, particularly in the workplace, adding an extra layer of complexity to their experiences.[2] In my own journey, I was acting *as if*, rather than embracing genuine authenticity. My focus on external validation was detrimental, rejecting my true self and unintentionally undermining my own goals.

Since leaving that position, being more direct has become a muscle I consistently work to strengthen. The more I exercise it, the more comfortable it feels, especially when speaking with the people I trust and love. Though my mom might not have encouraged it as a child, now, in tough conversations, she pushes me, "Just say it." This shift reflects an evolution in our relationship and marks my growth in tackling difficult conversations openly. I am pushing towards radical candor in every area of my life – in my friendships, marriage, and career.

MOVING IN STEP WITH MY SOUL

Today, I consider myself self-congruent, or living more authentically, with alignment between my thoughts, words, and actions. This has allowed me to prioritize self-love and quality time with friends and family while genuinely enjoying my work. The journey to this point required taking meaningful risks and asking key questions of myself, for instance, what does my energy feel like today?

Recognizing the impact of language, I consciously shifted from *hoping* to *trusting* and cultivated a mindset centered on gratitude. This change in perspective has redirected my focus toward accepting what *is* rather than fixating on what *could be*. I've kicked the habit of staying in toxic environments. Instead, I've learned to pause, quiet the noise, and listen to my inner voice. This allows me to connect with my thoughts and feelings and then articulate my needs and perspectives. Finding my voice has empowered me to express what I want, not assuming people can read my mind.

Reflecting on times like when I accepted that job against my gut instincts, I realize I've always had an intuition guiding me to listen and pause, even though I haven't consistently followed through. There were moments when I knowingly walked into situations that didn't align with my true self. Each of these experiences, however, served as valuable lessons. Ignoring my intuition feels unnatural—lacking sincerity and safety, breeding discomfort and weightiness. It feels like wearing armor as I dedicate time and energy to overthinking and overanalyzing, yet never feel I've done enough. Over time, I've gained the wisdom to gracefully walk away from situations that no longer serve me.

But when it's right, it's *really* right. In moments of alignment, everything falls seamlessly into place. It feels effortless. If only I could share this with my younger self, I would stress that this life is hers to live—she knows herself best, and no one can advocate for her more than she can. The world needs her unique voice, and she is inherently deserving of a life that makes her feel truly alive.

What I've learned through trial and error is that like many, my career path is not linear, and I thrive on creating new opportunities with extraordinary leaders. I now understand my optimal work environment is one with high levels of trust, respect, clear expectations, and outstanding performance – not a big-name company or fancy title. I flourish in spaces that prioritize psychological safety, foster open discussions, embrace failures as learning opportunities, promote innovation, and respect my boundaries as a wife and parent. When confronted with challenging decisions, I find a sense of belonging in environments where the choice is clear—upholding our principles and values over doubling revenue. This safety creates space for reflection and, ultimately, more meaningful contributions.

Breathwork and meditation are now important in my daily life to ease anxieties and tune in with myself. I'm also more focused on meaningful connections, coaching, and feedback. Actively investing in my relationships, I dedicate more time to my loved ones, being more present, and cherishing the joys of life with a toddler. As I navigate the world as an introvert with an extroverted child, I'm seeing the world in new ways and building more meaningful connections with those around me.

Recognizing that the people we trust often perceive us more clearly than we perceive ourselves, I value the role they play in revealing my blind spots. While receiving feedback is not always easy or comfortable, it is a critical aspect of my growth. By embracing feedback without defensiveness, I hold space for those I trust to shoot it to me straight. In contrast to my past tendency to turn inward and isolate during rough spots, I now work to connect both with myself and with others. Where I would previously fight fear with finding data and facts in pursuit of perfection, I take a beat, take a breath, and reach out for support.

Moving my body has always been important—whether it be yoga, dancing or taking boxing classes. This helps to declutter my thoughts, amplify my inner voice, and empower me to take confident and inspired action. With a clear mind and anxiety held at bay, I can then take that first step to tackle complicated projects, boosting my confidence and creating a constructive feedback loop. Prioritizing movement has become a cornerstone for my personal well-being and work performance.

SELF-DISCOVERY: A LIFELONG RHYTHM UNFOLDING

I am on the lifelong journey of discovering my true self and navigating what authenticity truly means for me. With more self-awareness and self-love, I feel empowered to embrace risks and stand firmly in my truth, recognizing that my values and perspectives are untethered to specific outcomes or external judgment. Instead, I am committed to showing up each day and offering my personal best, solely to fulfill my purpose, not others' expectations.

I revel in the newfound awareness of my personal power. This recommitment to myself influences how I show up in every aspect of life. I'm navigating the world with self-advocacy, unapologetically pursuing what I want without seeking permission. Embracing my wife's wisdom that "everything is *figureoutable*," I acknowledge life's challenges and am strategizing to bring my dreams to fruition, firmly knowing that my dreams are achievable, even if they look different from what I imagined. Standing in this space of self-empowerment is liberating, as I recognize that I am the master of my fate.

In spaces where worry and unspoken thoughts lingered, I now actively design a life that aligns with what I want. This journey of rediscovery feels akin to meeting my authentic self for the very first time, breathing life into a more vibrant existence where I am an active participant, not just a bystander. Loving and embracing myself for who I am has become the catalyst for sharing my unique gifts with the world, and in this transformative space, I'm finding peace.

I love it here.

As Brené Brown said, "You either walk into your story and own your truth, or you live outside of your story, hustling for your worthiness."[3] I am intentionally walking inside my story by using my unique strengths, steering clear of pursuing perfection or masking my true self. It is in this deliberate choice that effective leadership takes root—an authentic vulnerability emerges from an ongoing commitment to building self-awareness. It is in this mindfulness that we discover our limitless potential, influence, and genuine fulfillment.

The greatest gift I can give myself, extend to my son, and share with you is recognizing that everything you need is within you – you're writing your story. Your unique gifts are important, and your desires are meaningful.

Now take a deep breath. What is it that YOU truly want?

ABOUT THE AUTHOR

Sam Armstrong, an executive in government consulting, has forged a distinguished career marked by transformative leadership across various federal agencies. Drawing upon her expertise in strategic resource management, customer experience, change management, executive coaching, and benefits realization, Sam has been instrumental in spearheading impactful projects that reshape government and nonprofit landscapes.

Sam's professional journey includes tenures at renowned companies, and her educational foundation, laid at Emory University and The George Washington University, has been a cornerstone in her intellectual curiosity and professional development.

Dedicated to effecting positive change, Sam extends her influence beyond the boardroom. She serves on the boards of two local nonprofits – Words, Beats & Life and the Arlington County Fair. Additionally, she is a member of the Armed Forces Communications & Electronics Association (AFCEA) International Homeland Security Committee where she is dedicated to improving the health and security of our nation.

Growing up in an Air Force family, Sam's roots instilled in her a sense of service and community. Today, she lives in the Washington, DC area with her wife and son. Beyond her professional pursuits, Sam can be found enjoying live performances, embarking on travel adventures, and diving into the latest in fitness and wellness. Her multifaceted approach to life mirrors her commitment to living life on purpose and making a meaningful impact.

8

ANDREW BEAMON

EMPOWERING EXCELLENCE: FROM IMPOSTER SYNDROME TO AUTHENTIC LEADERSHIP

When people ask me about my career, I always say that there are many insights I wish I had possessed at the start of my journey. Through my experience navigating corporate America, I gained greater awareness of the pitfalls that hinder aspiring leaders from realizing their full potential. My aim is for my narrative to serve as a compass for both emerging young leaders embarking on their corporate paths and seasoned executives and entrepreneurs seeking renewed growth and expansion. By cultivating the appropriate mindset, we all can achieve corporate success while being our authentic selves.

TRANSITIONING TO THE BIG LEAGUES: FROM SMALL CITY TO CORPORATE CAREER CHALLENGES

I remember being out with my mother in my hometown, Waterbury, Connecticut, shopping at a discount retail store to find some business clothes. I had just landed my first corporate job, and I was in urgent need of a more polished business wardrobe as I prepared to transition to Washington, D.C. I certainly didn't want to look like I was in the wrong place when I arrived to the office. I only owned one black untailored suit and a pair of black shoes that I used for my interview, so I reached out to my family for help. My cash was pretty low because I had bought a house two years earlier during the peak of the housing bubble. I was a proud young homeowner who was also house-poor. Thankfully one cousin gave me his over-sized pair of brown loafers with a big silver buckle on top. I thought they looked outdated, but I needed brown shoes, so I made them work. I wouldn't say I was ready for GQ magazine, but I was more than grateful to receive the clothing donations and the fresh new suit my mother bought me.

Coming from a small city with its share of economic struggles, I was excited to be finally entering into a corporate career. I was hired as a consultant to help organizations improve their workplace by providing human resource strategy and employee engagement services for executives. I felt like I had finally made it. I was called up from the minor league to the major league. I'm sure most people can relate to that feeling when you either finally made the high school varsity team, were admitted to the college you were hoping for, or got that promotion and raise you long-awaited. I was on cloud nine! This was my shot (like the song from the Hamilton play), and I was not going to throw it away. Ultimately, this career transition would turn out to be more stressful and challenging than I anticipated, with a heavy dose of imposter syndrome greeting me at every turn.

THE CORPORATE AMERICA PITFALL: IMPOSTER SYNDROME

I began my new company's consulting orientation boot camp. All newly hired consultants go through a three-month training. It was a full week once a month at the world headquarters. The headquarters was a beautiful, state-of-the-art building right on the river. It was nothing like I had experienced before. The classrooms and offices were filled with bright leaders from all around the world. My colleagues showed up suited and booted in impressive business attire. Some of them graduated from top MBA schools, and others had experience working for other prestigious organizations. I was starting to feel less and less like the fearless Hamilton figure.

Navigating through class assignments and homework seemed effortless to others, yet for me, it demanded every ounce of effort to merely keep pace. I recall my heart racing each time the spotlight turned to me to answer a question. My fear wasn't just of providing an incorrect answer, it extended to the possibility of encountering smirks or laughter in response. Consequently, my participation dwindled, I asked fewer questions, and it felt too daunting to challenge any established ideas.

This fear of making mistakes carried over into my social interactions. During breakfast and lunch with colleagues, I refrained from sharing much about myself or engaging in casual conversation out of fear of saying something socially awkward. Slowly, I found myself becoming unrecognizable and my presence diminishing. It felt like I was gradually being buried alive in a sea of emotions, questioning my ability and wondering if I truly belonged. I thought maybe I wasn't smart enough, and I most likely would be on my way back to my hometown, working at my old job very soon.

Have you ever had a time when you felt you weren't enough? When self-doubt began to take you over? Or you felt like a fake? I was having a major case of imposter syndrome, a psychological occurrence when people doubt their talent, skills, and previous accomplishments and have a persistent internal fear of being exposed as a fraud.

What I know now that I wish I had known then, is that imposter syndrome is normal. According to the International Journal of Behavioral Science, 70% of people feel imposter syndrome at some point.[1] Their study also shares that the percentage may be even higher for executives and entrepreneurs, as well as people of color and other marginalized communities. In the moment, not only had I never heard of this term, I thought I was the only one grappling with this feeling. I learned later that many others in my orientation cohort shared the same experience. As an African-American man stepping into the corporate realm for the first time, these feelings of fear and self-doubt were significantly impacting my performance.

COMPARING YOURSELF TO OTHERS

This feeling of imposter syndrome was eating at me so much that I had to talk to someone. One night after finally completing a late-night group assignment, I said privately to my colleague, Greg, "*I don't know if I belong here. I don't think I'm going to make it. This boot camp is so overwhelming. Dan, Amy, Taj, and Jason always seem to ask brilliant questions. Their presentations are phenomenal, and they do incredible business case studies all while I'm banging my head up against the wall.*" It was embarrassing to admit that I felt intimidated, but I shared it anyway. I really didn't know Greg that well. A consulting firm can be a very competitive environment. If you are viewed as the top student in this training, you could be invited to high-profile projects, receive rewards and recognition, and be positioned to become a rainmaker (top revenue producer). On the other hand, if you are at the bottom of the pack, you may not have a very long future at the company.

Greg responded, "*Did you know that this orientation training is set up exactly like business school? Going through case studies and conducting 20-minute business consulting presentations isn't new to them. They have been practicing these consulting frameworks and business lingo (or jargon) their entire time at business school. Yes, they are impressive, but it came with time, practice, and training. And the other guy, Dan, yes, he is an amazing presenter, and keeps winning every presentation contest, but did you know he was a child actor? Not taking anything away from his business skills but of course he could present well, he has been performing in front of large crowds his entire life! Don't be so hard on yourself and don't give up, you'll be just fine.*"

I felt the stress, embarrassment, and disappointment release from my body. Despite the competitive nature of this training program, Greg took the time to reignite my confidence. I was more aware of why I felt these insecurities, and I was ready again to get back to business. I received Greg's message and I translated it as: **my problem is that I'm spending too much time comparing** *myself to others, and trying to figure out how to deliver my work like others. I need to be patient with my growth, and spend more time focusing on my natural talents and strengths. This company brought me here and hired me for a reason.*

This conversation helped direct me on the right path and re-ignite my confidence, but if you told me that in less than two years I would be leading consulting teams, managing successful employee engagement projects for several healthcare systems, and delivering executive presentations across the country, I would've said you were crazy. I think back and can't believe I almost gave up.

Comparing yourself to others will drive you crazy and lead you into a deep state of imposter syndrome. To counter this, I began shifting my approach from comparing to complementing. I began seeking opportunities to contribute my distinct value, aiming to complement the talents of my colleagues. I discovered that while most others had grandiose "pie in the sky" ideas, my strength was my knack for effective execution, developed through my prior role as a front-line manager. My proficiency in translating concepts into practical actions, and my hands-on understanding of real-world operations – distinct from theoretical discussions in the classroom or boardroom – emerged as a significant asset.

THE MYTH OF THE LONE HERO

The myth of the lone hero is another fallacy that many in corporate America believe to their detriment. In history class and throughout American culture, we celebrate the greatest of individuals, not groups. We grow up learning about the genius of people like Thomas Edison, Martin Luther King Jr., and others. As kids, most of us were never taught that the greats actually had a lot of help. Thomas Edison had a team of inventors he partnered with and he developed his skills by contributing to great inventions and teams before his big break. Mahalia Jackson prompted Martin Luther King Jr. during his speech at the 1963 March on Washington when she yelled to him from behind the podium, "Tell them about the dream, Martin," where he then put down the notes from the speech he prepared and began what we now know as the famous "I Have a Dream" speech. Even fictional movies kept the myth of the lone hero alive. I grew up watching movies like *Rambo*, with one superhero single-handedly winning a war for America. The legends and myths we are taught growing up have contributed to so many people at all stages of their career journey suffering from imposter syndrome. This myth could have an even more profound impact on women of color, given that the majority of celebrated individual accomplishments tend to center around those of white men.

The secret is this – **Greatness is seldom achieved in isolation**. In the initial phases of my corporate career and life overall, I mistakenly took pride in proclaiming that I accomplished everything independently. However, as I engaged in conversations with fellow corporate professionals, the veil over this truth began to lift. A few months into the consulting job, I sought guidance from a seasoned senior consultant, often referred to as a "rockstar," on how to better analyze my healthcare client's employee engagement survey results. After generously imparting his brilliant technique, I asked him how he learned to do this so well. His nonchalant response resonated deeply: "*I asked for help, and someone guided me – just as I've done for you.*"

Extending assistance to others, focusing on complementing others rather than comparing, and being unafraid to seek guidance played pivotal roles in charting my course to success in corporate America. Yet, the most crucial aspect of my new approach was simply **trusting myself**. Trusting in my authentic self has proven to be the most effective strategy, fostering not only resilience but also prosperity in my career.

How would you define your authentic self? Are you bringing your whole self to your work? How are you leveraging your natural talents to make an impact?

MY EVOLUTION: LEADERSHIP TRANSFORMATION

Reflecting on my evolution as a leader, I underwent a profound transformation when I began to trust my authentic self and cultivate my resourcefulness. This newfound confidence not only revolutionized my approach to leadership but also empowered me to deliver impactful community and employee engagement programs.

For instance, in the aftermath of Superstorm Sandy, my consultancy was tasked with the vital mission of supporting the recovery efforts of small businesses in New Jersey. Leading a dedicated team of small business mentors, many of whom were retired senior executives, we initially encountered resistance in our efforts to provide disaster preparedness workshops and one-on-one mentoring. Recognizing the disconnect, I engaged with community leaders and attentively listened to the feedback of business owners. It became apparent that our approach failed to address the community's most pressing need – financial assistance.

Convincing my seasoned team to change our strategy was a challenge, yet I remained steadfast in my conviction that it was necessary for true community impact. This shift towards a focus on financial assistance proved pivotal, enabling us to effectively aid the recovery efforts by assisting hundreds of small business owners through the complex application process of the New Jersey Economic Development Authority's grants and loans recovery program. Through our leveraging of existing resources and partnerships, we addressed the community's most urgent need. My ability to confidently challenge our initial approach, despite the team's small business experience, was instrumental in driving this transformation.

Similarly, during the COVID-19 pandemic, my adaptability and resilience shone through in my approach to driving employee engagement. Originally designed as an in-person initiative, the employee engagement program I spearheaded aimed to bring together corporate employee volunteers in supporting local nonprofit executive teams by providing their professional expertise in areas such as strategy, branding, marketing, and accounting. When the pandemic struck, there were calls from senior executives to cancel this nationwide program. However, recognizing the pressing need to support struggling nonprofits during these trying times, I saw an opportunity not only to bolster the company's reputation and brand but also to provide colleagues with a source of excitement amid the physical isolation and uncertainty.

Instead of succumbing to the pressure to cancel the program in the face of pandemic restrictions, I successfully advocated its continuation by transitioning it to a virtual platform. This transformation not only widened employee participation but also enabled collaboration across geographic boundaries in ways we had never experienced previously. As a result, the virtual format enhanced employee networking opportunities and encouraged cross-departmental partnerships.

These examples highlight the vital role of innovation in elevating engagement initiatives, which was made achievable through trusting myself – my abilities and values. Throughout these experiences, my resourcefulness has been a testament to my perseverance and problem-solving abilities. This journey has paved the way for a career marked by successful leadership of teams, navigation of complex projects, and development of strategic partnerships, ultimately driving impactful change in both community and employee engagement initiatives.

CALL TO ACTION: EMBRACE THE LEADER WITHIN

While I consider resourcefulness and resilience vital leadership talents, I encourage you to embark on a journey of self-discovery and reflect on your own natural leadership abilities. Evolve into the leader you are uniquely designed to be. Challenge yourself to cultivate and sustain success as a leader.

When I'm asked about my definition of corporate success, I emphasize that it transcends the attainment of C-suite positions, impressive titles, or organizational prestige. True success lies in giving your utmost, leveraging your unique talents, making a meaningful impact, challenging the status quo, and unwaveringly upholding your integrity. How will you measure your success?

As you navigate the unpredictable landscape of your corporate career, remember this – **authenticity is your greatest strength**. Human beings are not designed to replicate others. It's draining to mimic others or maintain a false image. Instead, uncover your unique talents and be resilient in the face of challenges.

Your journey is a marathon, not a sprint. Be a change agent, lead with humility, and never forget that true success is being proud of the authentic work you contribute to the world. So, stand tall, show up as a leader, and forge a path that reflects the genuine, empowered, and impactful individual that you are meant to be. This mindset will not only assist you in successfully navigating corporate America but, more importantly, in living a life you can be proud of.

ABOUT THE AUTHOR

Andrew Beamon is a leadership and organizational development consultant with close to 20 years of experience in the non-profit and corporate sector, where he has helped organizations build and improve their employee engagement, corporate citizenship, and diversity, equity, & inclusion strategies and programs.

Andrew is currently the founder and CEO of AB Consulting, and the author of the Amazon best-seller, "From Promises To Progress: A leadership guide to help organizations avoid common mishaps and bring their racial equity aspirations to life."

He began his career as a management consultant before transitioning to nonprofit field operations, and eventually, a senior leader for a global financial institution's U.S. corporate citizenship team.

Andrew's mission is to help organizations bring their values and purpose to life through meaningful and intentional actions. He has shared his work with many audiences, including The Black Executive Perspective podcast, National Association of Black Accountants of Connecticut, Vital Voices, NAACP National Convention, and the Congressional Black Caucus Annual Leadership Conference.

Andrew received his bachelor's degree in business with a concentration in hospitality and tourism administration from North Carolina Central University in Durham, North Carolina. He received his Master's degree in organizational psychology from the

University of Hartford in Hartford, Connecticut, and he has completed Georgetown's Strategic Diversity & Inclusion Management Executive Certification and Boston College's Certification in Strategic Corporate Citizenship Management.

https://andrewbeamon.com/

9

ANGELA DIXON WILLIAMS

THE BLUEPRINT OF AUTHENTIC LEADERSHIP

This chapter is dedicated to my mother; I have always drawn inspiration from you.

∽

Awareness is the space where the mind falls back to allow your heart and soul to breathe, consuming the openness of the universe, experiencing transformation, and nurturing wisdom. Awareness invites consciousness to experience vulnerability laced with a litany of emotions. Awareness takes us deeper into the essence of consciousness; here, we must confront ourselves at the core of who we are and what we project into the world.

— ANGELA D. WILLIAMS, 2024

I didn't always have these words to articulate what awareness meant to me. Instead, I knew that stillness and the ability to quiet my mind gave me a sense of clarity, peace, and spiritual connection. It wasn't until I experienced a disruption in my ability to tap into this quiet space that I gained a more profound understanding of its power.

Until now, I reserved sharing the story of my corporate climb. Even co-workers, friends, and family present in my life at the time have little insight into this journey's emotional and physical impact. I have since learned that on the other side of awareness is transformation and a calling to share these experiences with others.

HOMEMADE RESILIENCE

I was born into a family with incredible drive and grit. For over 20 years, my mother worked in a steaming hot sewing factory five to six days a week. She cooked our family meals and maintained our household. Stretching her industrial seamstress salary, she paid for two homes. Calling out sick, leaving work early, or taking a real vacation was a rarity. She embodied her belief of working twice as hard as anyone else, striving to be the best at everything she set out to achieve. She was a loyal employee, took pride in her hard work, and was meticulous with her craft. She supported her children unconditionally and was a committed and faithful friend—a leader in her own right.

When I entered the workforce, my mother's leadership was the blueprint for *"how"* I approached life and work. When my son was born, he inspired my motivation for the *"why."* At first sight, I vowed to love him unconditionally. I pledged his father would always be in his life, and we would work to acquire financial resources to ensure his access to experiences and education, surpassing the privileges of his parents. He was my reason to grind! My "how" and "why" were ingrained in how I approached the corporate world, but those years weren't without challenges or missed steps.

CULTIVATING WISDOM

I had a natural craving to understand the connections within organizations. I was intrigued by the complexity of internal operations and external influences. How did these corporate systems work, and why? My curiosity stems from my early childhood when people-watching and listening to people's stories was one of my favorite things.

It seemed almost everyone in our family could deliver an award-winning account of life experiences at the drop of a dime. Like audiobooks, they carried a library of tales and truths. Often, I would eavesdrop and listen for any chance of a captivating narrative of history, drama, or a wise tale. Intently, I watched them display waves of emotion and even comedic gestures. As they spoke, I imagined an active stage filled with vibrant characters.

My capacity to observe the inner qualities of organizations, how leaders lead, and how workers work is not a fluke. I perceive work as a different stage, but a stage, nonetheless. Always in the back of my mind was the internalized childhood script to work harder, be smarter, look the part, and refrain from showing emotions at work. Honestly, the replay of those ideas was synonymous with finding a stable job where I would work for thirty years, retire, and live happily ever after— I call this the thirty-year plan.

Fast forward fifteen years into my career as a global humanitarian government program consultant, collaborating with overseas entities, government agencies, and non-government partners. There were several eye-opening moments during this time in my career. By now, I had traveled to exciting places and held two assistant director positions running programs outside the country and in US territory.

On more than one occasion, I opted to take a lower position and a pay cut for the promise of future promotion. When negotiating my worth failed, my default was to mimic my mother's blueprint of working twice as hard to prove I was worthy of the position and the compensation. Once hired, I had a track record of advancing within an organization. Still, the trade-off of taking a step back for the promise of future growth validated the message that " more is required." Internally, this stirred up the repetitive self-talk of *whether I was good enough. And, am I working hard enough?*

A SPACE TO THRIVE

I recall one mid-career opportunity when leadership asked me to run a program on an island in the Pacific Ocean. Honored and humbled that they thought of me, I worked tirelessly to make the program successful. My work on that island was a huge accomplishment for me, the community we served, and the organization.

Despite the accolades from our senior leaders and partners, my boss made it clear upon my return to headquarters that advancement within that organization wasn't in my future. She expressed no plans to leave her job, nor did she foresee her boss departing anytime soon. She went on to ask, "What will you do next"? Of course, her words caught me off guard. This interaction felt like a stake-your-claim move and a real-life representation of the "glass cliff." I felt bullied, and the impact was profound.

This experience opened my eyes to the diversity of the leadership landscape across the entire field. There weren't any leaders around who looked like me to reach out to; only a handful worked in the field. I never spoke about my boss's comments because I doubted the leaders above her would understand the magnitude of what she said. Instead, it was time for me to move on. Within three months, I joined another organization, accepting a more junior role with a pay cut. Hitting the reset button, I again set out to prove my talents.

After receiving several promotions, I finally landed a stable mid-level leadership position with a six-figure salary comparable to the role. I was in a fantastic place mentally, physically, and spiritually. We had the home, two cars, and could pay for our son's college tuition. According to the blueprint, this was it—I had done all the things! My happily ever after was less than fifteen years away. The thirty-year plan might have manifested if my perspective on work and my leadership capacity hadn't started to transform.

THE POWER OF PRESENCE

My formula for success was investing time into my team, continuous learning, and understanding how to tap into the potential of our individual and collective strengths. I had learned to flex my leadership style to the needs of each of the managers on my team. We conquered lots of "first-time" experiences, projects, and tasks. A pivotal one for me was our first team offsite. I hosted the event at home, footing the bill for the expenses. Everyone has memories of this event. The one that I frequently reflect on is a seemingly insignificant moment that changed my career trajectory.

It was the first session of the offsite. The team was sitting on the screened porch, and I was standing near the flipchart, ready to scribe the notes. We began to discuss how we had worked so hard to establish ourselves within the organization. From the team's perspective, the other groups weren't pulling their weight. I had just finished reading a book by Eckhardt Tolle. It was a complex read, and while I only understood about a third of the book, at the time, I recognized the ego-driven energy of our conversation—it wasn't a good feeling.

I decided to engage the team in an exercise to release the negative energy. As they voiced their complaints, I listed their thoughts on what the other teams should or shouldn't do on opposite sides of the flipchart. Then, we worked through the list to determine if our team could change or influence the outcome of any of the items presented. If we could change an item— we created a task. All the other items fell outside our sphere of influence and were out of our control.

The vibe shifted, our pace slowed, and we were more productive. I explained the importance of observation and influence, describing how I had used the opening activity to assess the teams' perspectives coming into the offsite. I then shared examples of replicating this behavior both individually and as a team. Until now, despite my accomplishments, I was unsure of myself as a leader, but the moment of synchronicity among the team made me recognize the leader within me.

STEPPING INTO LEADERSHIP

One day, the client entered my office frustrated and concerned about a project delay. My boss continuously ignored her complaints. She believed he was losing interest and maybe it was time for him to retire. She was also unsure if anyone in the organization was ready to take his place, and bringing someone in from the outside would be risky. Before I could pull back the words, I heard myself say, "I am ready." My heart skipped a beat or two at the shock of hearing those words fill the room. She hadn't considered me for the role, but her facial expression indicated she was seriously contemplating my declaration.

Shortly after our conversation, the client returned with a plan to create a deputy position as an interim transition. My boss, the Program Manager/Vice President, was set to retire within the next year. In the meantime, he agreed to mentor me as his successor. Now, the challenge is, do I choose door number one? It's the safer option. My team and I are at the top of our game, and staying in my current position aligns with the thirty-year plan. I had established myself as a subject matter expert; even if we lost the contract, I would likely receive an offer to join the incumbent firm. Or do I pick door number two? It's by far the riskier option fraught with unknowns. I would eventually assume the leadership responsibility for a team that was formerly my peers. Could I gain their respect and trust in this capacity? Did I want this responsibility? Could I do the job? Will I get the support I need? I had so many questions.

In my mind, a third option existed. Maybe I could help my boss see the light. We could rebuild the client relationship and steer the program back on track with each of us remaining secure in our roles. But he hadn't asked for my help, and all attempts failed miserably. Similarly, as I transitioned into the deputy role, the mentoring from my boss didn't go well. The sessions were nothing more than a check-the-box exercise. As I stood cluelessly witnessing the day's rant, he ripped the mentoring certificate to pieces before me. That gesture pretty much describes my transition journey.

I had become accustomed to handling the audacious and subtle aggressions experienced in the workplace over the years. I extended empathy, respect, loyalty, and grace to people in spaces where these virtues sometimes went unreciprocated. I chose to minimize my attention to these behaviors, grateful for the lesson of how and how not to lead.

Determined to be the leader I wanted to experience, I immersed myself in the deputy role. Focusing on the vision for overseeing the entire organization, I began preparing my team for the domino effect of advancement opportunities resulting from my promotion. When it was time to step into the new position, our corporate business director and client promised I would have the necessary support to succeed. Yet, even with this commitment, my title and compensation were below that of my predecessor and peers. It would take over a year to secure market parity.

Oh, and there was another surprise. Our client retired shortly after my promotion, and the business director left the organization. For the first four months, I was responsible for overseeing the entire operations without the support of those roles.

THE CALM BEFORE THE STORM

Every organization experiences disruptions. After an almost three-year run of record-breaking performance ratings, the tide shifted. Events equating to utter chaos followed. Globally, the program wasn't moving fast enough for the powers that be, so they sent an entire task force of help to the hub. Pile on the utopian expectation of integrating an entirely new team and culture into the mix of the insatiable demands for growth and productivity. Then, encapsulate these conditions into a polarizing environment where mission versus non-mission-driven activities cloud the organization's strategy, priorities, and operational norms. And there you have it, the formula for a perfect storm.

The space where I had once tapped into grounding myself and silencing the noise was collapsing under the immense pressures of work. *How Am I Enough When More Is Always Needed?* The infinite nature of "more" had tipped the scale. Guiding the organization without support fueled the turmoil brewing within me. The convergence of work disruptions with my physical, mental, and spiritual dissonance amplified the storm. I was exhausted from defending everything from program priorities, the size of my office, recruiting talent, equitable compensation—and— wildly enough, my new car.

The undercutting actions and remarks hit differently in the rawness of the grander scheme of constantly striving to be enough. Even successful individuals can feel uncertain and vulnerable at times. While leaders and networks can play a pivotal role in creating space to encourage others to speak out when facing these challenges, the absence of cultural sensitivity, psychological safety, and the support structures that create a fair and inclusive workplace can contribute to the ills of an employee's well-being.

AT THE TOP OF THE CLIFF, CAUGHT IN A STORM

When it happens to you, it is like being engulfed by the winds of a category-five hurricane. Oh, shit! Is this me? For months, I had dragged myself out of bed for work that was once my livelihood. With the sun still hidden, I glanced at my reflection while grooming myself for work. Back and forth from the bathroom into the dimly lit bedroom, I tipped quietly to avoid disrupting my husband's sleep. I put on my work clothes and slid into my car to begin the twenty-minute commute to work.

But— this day was different—I was confused. Staring at myself in the mirror, I said out loud, "Is that me?" I mean, it had to be, right? The reflection in the mirror looked like an aged, exhausted, depleted, and sickly version of me. My shoulders slumped, and my body ached all over— "This job is going to kill me," I thought.

Now, I am far from the dramatic type, but at that moment, I 100% believed this job was about to take me out. I was overwhelmed and afraid of becoming another woman who had fallen from a sudden and fatal stress-induced heart attack or stroke.

My work days were intense. Every day, to get a head start, I arrived at the office hours before anyone else. There was always an urgency, a line of people waiting to speak to me, and a calendar full of meetings. With every hour packed with activities, working through lunch was the norm. An occasional glimpse of sunbeams hitting my office window was the extent of my exposure to daylight. After putting in 10, 15, and sometimes 18-plus hour days, dinner versus sleep was always a dilemma. With morning only a few hours away, the preference for sleep usually prevailed.

At that moment, *I Hated My Job; I* didn't recognize myself, my husband was insensitive, my mother was dying of Alzheimer's, my church was undergoing a scandal, and if I am being honest, *I Hated Life*. At the top of the glass cliff, the reflection in the mirror was unrecognizable. Who could I share this vulnerable feeling of my value being only as good as the next crisis or problem I could solve?

Nearing my wit's end, I typed up my resignation and prayed my desire to send it would disappear. My loyalty and fixer tendencies hadn't completely abandoned me. I latched on to a raindrop of hope that working even harder would rekindle my passion for this work. The eternal optimist in me held on for six months until the visceral pit in my stomach was unbearable. It was time to let go.

AT THE HEART OF IT ALL

Advancing in that organization was a road of successes, challenges, and sacrifices. My story contains intricate layers of leaning into existing structures of organizations with stewardship, resilience, and perseverance. While my "work ethic" might resemble the famous discourse of popular culture, equally important is the acknowledgment of my personal experiences with self-doubt and self-worth. There was an emotional expense of navigating workplace obstacles. The underlying narrative slowly unfolds the imprint of deeply rooted burnout and trauma.

My humanity urges me to call out the construction of barriers that exist in the workplace. Humility allows me to reflect internally on my personal growth, asking myself existential questions to reconcile my "life at work" with my life's purpose. The healing was a winding path of coaching, education, meditation, prayer, reading, therapy, and a long list of self-care modalities. Yet, it was the epiphany of someone else's story resonating with my own experiences, which prompted a deeper exploration of my insights.

In an intimate setting of no more than ten women leaders from my community, I listened to the president of a Fortune 500 company describe her work experience. She talked about her organization's demonstrated values of diversity and inclusion. She described mentoring relationships and a supportive work environment where she courageously called out challenges and disparate practices. She mentioned one particular leader at her company who was an inspiring champion throughout her career. Empowered to embrace her authenticity, she attributed much of her ability to thrive and build a successful career to never losing sight of being herself.

NURTURE THE CORE OF WHO YOU ARE

Pausing to reflect on the stories baked into my narrative slowly surfaced the layers underneath my experiences. The stillness of looking inward revealed feelings of uncertainty and vulnerability when the outward layers paint a picture of success. Operating in constant survival mode while navigating stubborn corporate cultures and internal beliefs isn't the same as thriving. Admittedly, those survival behaviors had served me well until they overshadowed my self-compassion. My creativity, perspective, and confidence were shrinking. That pivotal moment of not recognizing myself in the mirror was a nudge. It had been too long since I checked in with my authentic self.

Sharing a glimpse into this chapter of my life illuminates the transformative power of awareness. My healing journey was infused with encounters of signals and signs, nudging, pushing, and sometimes pulling me to *revise* my blueprint, *refine* my narrative, *and recharge my* authenticity. We can all benefit from finding the compassion and stillness to delve deeper into our narratives. I invite you to start your journey today—our collective exploration can inspire and normalize the nurturing of our genuine well-being.

ABOUT THE AUTHOR

Meet Angela Dixon Williams—a devoted advocate for conscious leadership. Angela has held various leadership roles, from steering multifaceted programs to leading policy and IT implementation. Her journey began with a deep-rooted belief in prioritizing people alongside business strategies. Early in her career, Angela adopted the mantra of "pour into your people, and they will pour into the success of the organization." This philosophy became the cornerstone of her approach to leadership development, organizational transformation, and diversity, equity, and inclusion practices. Angela's leadership is characterized by integrity, empathy, and a relentless commitment to excellence.

Angela's dedication to continuous learning and best practices has enhanced her role as a consultant and coach across federal, nonprofit, and commercial sectors. With a bachelor's degree in business administration from the University of Maryland, a master's degree in organizational development from Pepperdine University, and certifications in Diversity, Equity, and Inclusion from Georgetown University, Angela's expertise is matched by her commitment to personal growth.

Beyond her professional pursuits, Angela is on a personal mission to redefine leadership. She believes that leading from the heart creates a boundless space for growth where unlimited potential resides. Angela Williams isn't just rewriting the playbook on leadership; she's providing the blueprint for unlocking your authentic leadership potential.

PART III

RESILIENCE & TRANSFORMATION

"When life hands you a difficult situation where you feel undervalued and disrespected, be bold and brave enough to know your worth."

— YAI VARGAS

10

TRINI K. SHERMAN

WISDOM THROUGH THE PIVOTS

It is September 2018, and it feels like the weight of the world is on my shoulders. My mother is dying. My children need me. My marriage is in decay. My company is draining the life out of me. I am drowning. And I don't know if I am going to make it. I am really afraid!

WISDOM NUG #1: KNOW WHEN IT'S TIME TO PIVOT.

I am sitting in the recliner my mother always sat in to watch television and keep up with worldly news. My body is sending a blaring warning signal that carrying this heavy load is not sustainable. The room feels like it is shifting. I am lightheaded. *Why does my watch say my heartbeat is at 123 bpm? I am sitting with my mother, not working out, so what is going on?* Fear grips me as I reflect on the fact that my mother, father, maternal and paternal grandmothers all suffered from cardiovascular disease in different forms. I am now concerned about my own heart health and mortality. This is a wake-up call! A moment of awareness. An invitation for a pivot. What will I do?

While watching my mother lay there, in the bed supplied by hospice, a shell of herself, no longer able to care for herself, I know the end is coming. This proud, independent, successful woman who I admire now depends on all of us to care for her every need. This is hard to watch. Her frail body tells a story of our humanity and the inevitable deterioration promised. Sometimes, I have to turn away emotionally, withdraw to my logic, make plans, do things, anything not to feel. But now, in an instant, there is nowhere to hide because death has become very real for me. Even though my family owned a funeral business and I had attended numerous funerals, even those of family members, death was never more real than coming face to face with my own mortality. "Trini, you are going to die one day," I said to myself. "If you continue to live this way and get to the end of life, will you be satisfied?" The answer was a resounding "NO."

"NO," because there were dreams inside of me, hopes for love that felt good, people I wanted to help, and lightness I wanted to feel. I wanted to see who I could be without all the heaviness I carried, all the pain, the hurt, the disappointment for life choices I had made while giving in to external influences that had denied me my truest desires. That late evening in September 2018, I became aware that I had a choice to make: would I continue the path I was on or would I pivot and choose something different? Something had to change, but what and how?

WISDOM NUG #2: CHOOSING YOU IS NOT SELFISH.

My marriage was at the top of the list of things that had to change. We had been married for almost twenty-seven years and dated for four years. The infidelity, harsh words, confusion of how love could hurt so bad, asking God "Why me?", self-blame, embarrassment, shame, and loss of hope had thundered a clear message for many years that this relationship needed to end. I did not have the heart to divorce while my children were young. I had concerns for the impact on our families, our Christian community, and how I would be able to live with the failure. Being the high-achiever who cannot fail, I had to give it everything I had until I knew in my soul the end had come. With all of that, I was angry with myself for being in this situation. It was not as though I didn't have signs when we dated in college. It wasn't like the writing wasn't on the wall after college. It was always right there in my face, yet here I was, lost and confused. What could I do to make this better because failure was not an option? Or was it?

In July 2018, we postponed a cruise because my mother had taken a turn for the worse. Death appeared to be imminent, so we rescheduled the cruise for October 2018, near our 27th wedding anniversary. This trip, for me, was one last try at turning the corner to a better relationship. I feel like I said that audibly at the time, and for sure, I knew it in my soul. I had to give it one last shot. I had poured so much of my life out in those 27 years and endured so much. I always wanted my children to have a family unit with a mother and father who loved and cherished each other while pouring the best into them. How could I fail them? So, I continued to work, pray, and hope for better. Although I endured a lot, the mother in me provided the strength to stay the course. However, I knew the end of the road was approaching and approaching with a vengeance.

With a vengeance? My mom's health had been on a steady decline since July 2018, but she was a fighter and was still with us as the rescheduled cruise approached. A couple of weeks prior to the cruise, Mom became so restless and agitated that the hospice nurse suggested she go into respite care so a physician could evaluate her needs and make recommendations to keep her safe with her having very limited mobility. She had to be transported by ambulance to the hospice care center while I followed behind in my car. What in the world is going on? I had traveled behind an ambulance many nights as she was being taken to the emergency room through the years. This was different. This was hospice. This was about impending death. I did not know how to handle this reality except to be strong, take care of business, and keep moving. As I got Mom settled in, she begged me not to leave her there. She would grab my hand and with a soft whisper ask me to take her home. "Let's go home, Trini," she would say while she tried to move her leg out of the bed. Her mind thought she was moving, but I could see her legs were going nowhere. Her mind was not aware that her body was failing her. Watching that, feeling the responsibility for her care and carrying the burden of guilt for bringing her there, broke my heart. Still, I did not know how to express what I was feeling. Suppressing negative or heavy emotions was my pattern and here it was in full force.

I no longer knew how to safely take care of Mom at home. While she had always asked if she could transition this life from home and not in a hospital, I was not sure from what the medical professionals said that she would make it back home. Will she still be here when it's time for the cruise? Will I carry guilt if she cannot return home prior to the end? Was I being selfish? How much more could I take and not break under the stress? I was not sure and made the decision to allow this respite process to unfold organically.

Being the strong, determined woman that she was, Mom lived a few more weeks, and the time for the cruise was upon us. I was torn between my desire for a break, the need to look into my marriage away from the rigors of family and business, and being there for my mother. For many months now, I had been feeling this deep calling to do what I wanted to do, when I wanted to do it, and how I wanted to do it. I was ready for a level of freedom, all things my way. But was this selfish? That is how it felt at times, but the desire for autonomy never dissipated. This was a crossroads of sorts; would I choose what was best for me or give in to the guilt of being a "good" daughter? My brother, nephew, and the hospice staff took great care of her while I was gone. I chose ME!

WISDOM NUG #3: YOU CANNOT RUN FROM THE TRUTH.

With determination and hope in hand, I stepped out on faith and embarked on a Caribbean cruise. The break was great, and the pampering of the staff was just what I needed. Massages, good food all day long, no responsibilities. The rest, the sunshine, the fresh air and open seas, Yes! I loved the vastness of the sea as I looked out over the horizon. The unlimited possibilities that exist, the sunsets, the ripples of the ocean and the safety of the large ship, as swimming in deep water is a real fear for me.

While there were moments of enjoyment, I still felt limited, dealing with some of the same issues from home – feeling stuck in a place too small for the me God created. This was a soul awareness. No matter the good times of the week, the reality of "more" stared me dead in the eye. I wanted more! Leaving the country and sailing the seas did not change that reality.

WISDOM NUG #4: THERE IS A HIGH PRICE TO PAY FOR NOT STAYING TRUE TO SELF.

Reality followed me home. My marriage was still on life-support. My mother could no longer eat, speak, or move. Thankfully, we were able to bring her home for her transition nearly two weeks after our return. My mother left my touch on November 8, 2018.

What a day that was! Disobedience to myself years earlier came back to bite me. My husband and I, along with two partners, had bought a transportation company back in 2014. Prior to the purchase, we visited the office, and I knew immediately in my mind and soul that the Trini God created would not thrive in this environment. The office was disorganized, papers piled high, the furniture was dated, the transportation business was a foreign concept to me; nothing fit. I was a solid NO! So why did I agree to go along with my husband and partners? I was promised it would be a group effort, and the cultural expectation of the supportive wife won. Guess what happened? Ninety percent of the responsibility landed on my shoulders as I became President and Managing Partner, and they were inconsistent in their support.

Nonetheless, under my leadership, our fleet and staff doubled, and revenue grew by 70% in about three years. This might look like success, but to make that happen required 12-hour workdays and managing staff that did not have good work ethics. This was not the place for me. My stress level skyrocketed, sleepless nights were frequent, guilt for missing out on time with my youngest daughter, who was in high school, enveloped me, and now, on the day of my mother's transition, that disobedience was staring me in the face. No matter how hard I tried, I could not get home after I got a call around lunchtime from Mom's nurse informing me that her condition was deteriorating. In full disclosure, Mom had many days in the previous year that appeared to be the end, but she rebounded. All of those times, I could immediately drop everything and run to the emergency bell. Today, however, staffing issues made it impossible. I didn't get home until after 4:00 PM and quickly realized Mom was leaving us very soon.

Now, when I look back, I see the price I paid for my decision to purchase that company. Valuable time with my youngest daughter was sacrificed, I gained weight, my heart would race randomly, gray covered my hair, my focus was diluted in my mother's last days, and my dreams and visions had been deferred. What a high price to pay!

WISDOM NUG #5: CHANGE TAKES COURAGE.

Between my mother's death in November 2018 and the end of January 2019, the continuation of ugliness in my marriage made it crystal clear that now was the time to make a change. Courage would be required to no longer defer the dreams and visions I had for my life because my decision would have a ripple effect on the lives of those I loved. My oldest daughter was pregnant with my first grandchild and due in February 2019. My youngest daughter was graduating high school in June 2019. My nephew, who is like a son to me, was getting married in July of the same year. And here I was, contemplating divorce when all of these wonderful things were happening for my family. How could I make this decision now? Because NOW is when I knew it to be true. This is when I knew I was done. This is when I knew my future was brighter than my past, and it was up to me to go get it. I could have waited until after the wedding, and no one's "happy days" would have been impacted. I had done that for almost 27 years; putting off what I knew was best for me for the perceived needs of my family. My integrity said you cannot pretend you do not know the truth for yourself, so you must speak it now. I chose to face my fears, lean into courage, go after purpose, and trust God to take care of the rest.

I made the courageous decision in late January 2019 to inform my then-husband that I was divorcing him. For many years, I warned him that allowing me to get to the point that I was done, would result in no comebacks. No do-overs. No try-agains. Once I am done, I am done. I had given a lot of room for forgiveness, reconciliation, growth and development, and even grace. Now it was over, he accused me of blindsiding him, as well as a host of other things. Those hard words didn't matter; I was at peace with my decision and determined to find the best version of myself, no matter what was being said about me.

WISDOM NUG #6: IT STARTS WITH OBEDIENCE.

Divorcing after 28 years of marriage was challenging, and it was timely that I was invited to travel to Israel in March 2020. This was shortly after selling the business in January that year. The decision to sell is one I am so thankful for on a deep level. My faith, my intuition, and every fiber of my being told me in November 2019 to sell or close the business by January 2020. I thought it was because of the stress alone, but it was far more than that. Later the true blessing would be revealed.

I felt called to take that trip to Israel and determined if God allowed us to go, even though COVID was lurking around the world, I was going. My intuitive knower, that part inside of me that knows the right way, that soft voice of wisdom, was very strongly directing me. In my obedience, God met me there in the Jordan River. As I traversed into the Jordan River, each step I took resulted in a deeper feeling of tingling running through my body. A well of emotions rose, and once out of the water, all I could say with tears running down my face was, "It was the best thing ever." I know in my heart that God touched me deeply, and my life changed forever. This was the beginning of the internal work.

I returned home to a changed world! There were no paper towels or toilet tissue in the stores. In a week, borders were closed, and we were on lockdown. COVID was full-on! Thankful does not adequately explain what I felt when I realized my obedience to sell the company saved me from a business disaster. A transportation company would not have thrived during the lockdown. Daily waking to that realization reinforced the importance of intuition, prayer, and listening to the voice of God.

WISDOM NUG #7: NOTHING CAN STOP ME FROM BEING ME EXCEPT ME.

The time in lockdown gave space for me to figure out my next steps. Through prayer and discernment, I decided my next professional pursuit would be life coaching. This is where the deep internal work expanded. I looked inside, found old patterns, disrupted them, and created new ways of living. Cleansing a lot of the hurt opened the channels for the messages from my inner knower to be clearly heard. Today, my decisions are more empowered, and I feel more powerful than I knew possible.

Courage showed up in my decision to remove myself from a toxic marriage and in selling a company that robbed me of my greatest business resources. Because of these two decisions, I am empowered as a Certified Professional Coach to Elevate Women into the Fullness of Power and as the founder and host of a live-streaming show inspiring women into courageous action. I am a powerful example to my daughters to choose relationships that elevate them. My courageous decisions exemplify to women that you can pivot, start over, and make a better life for yourself.

I am a victor. A woman of purpose. I now know that I am on the path to complete satisfaction at the end of life because I am in the arena, giving it all I got, authentically and unapologetically Me. You are also powerful! You also have the power to face your challenges with courage and determination. Allow Awareness to be your guide. Take a look inside, determine what you want, and courageously make it happen. Fear will surely raise its ugly head, but trust and believe that when you take action, it loses its power. May you step boldly through awareness and into power with purpose. The world needs all of you, and I look forward to raising our voices together for a higher purpose.

ABOUT THE AUTHOR

Trini K. Sherman is a Certified Professional Coach, Founder of a Transformational Coaching Practice, host of her video podcast: Unbounded with Trini, and Expert in Unbounded Living and Overcoming Life Challenges.

Trini believes in the power within each of us to shape our life experiences, rooted in the truth of who we are. To be a beacon of light for her three daughters, she courageously pivoted from a toxic 28-year marriage, laying the foundation for her transformational coaching practice—supporting women globally to "Elevate into the Fullness of their Power."

Her story is one of overcoming challenges—divorce, growing up in a home with alcohol abuse, caregiving for parents, prioritizing others over herself, and leading a company not aligned with her desires. With strength and resilience, Trini crafted a blueprint to pivot into Unbounded Power—living on purpose, authentically, and positively impacting the world. Now living life on her terms, Trini leads the way for women to speak their truth, take center stage, and craft a story filled with pure joy and peace.

As a Certified Professional Coach, Trini guides others to break free from self-sabotage, reconnect with their true desires, and master the tools of Unbounded living. You can connect with Trini on

Email: Trini@unboundedwithtrini.com

11

NIKKI WALKER

STRONGER THAN PRIDE

MEETING THE MOMENT

Watershed moments. They have a way of moving you. I have emerged victoriously on the other side of them every time I've had one. I've been awash with notions, clarifying prophecies, and aha moments while wading through their waters. In its truest form, water not only cleanses but gives life to those who partake in its goodness. It is almost perfect in its liquid form, hydrating and nourishing humankind and all God's creations. Watershed moments are much like that. They nourish and cleanse the mind from doubt and regret. They offer you a clear mind on which to build pathways to the next level of success. Watershed moments are crucial, but only if you go with the flow. Fighting against a body of water, much like fighting against the weight of a watershed moment is futile. One writhes and struggles, fighting to breathe, to stay above water and alive. When you ride the inevitable wave; however, your strokes become powerful and meaningful, and you learn to float when it is time to be still.

I haven't always gone the way of the water. In fact, there have been times when I have fought against the watershed moments with all my might. You see, once you have the information, it becomes your responsibility to act on it *always* and in *all ways*. I've not always been so pliable that I would follow the direction given by the supernatural awareness distributed in waves during my watershed moments. But, as you live, you learn, and the charge becomes easier to accept. By leaning in, you become one with the movement taking place around you. Change, while inevitable, becomes less of a danger and more of an adventure where, in most cases, you are the hero. It's in these moments where you must take a minute to stand in your awareness and look from whence you've come. In these moments, you determine what to do with the truths bestowed upon you, and it is in these moments where all things are available to you, and all things are possible.

Over the past two and a half decades, I have experienced wealth and poverty on the same scale. I have laughed until I cried and cried until I'd run out of tears. My highs have been so lucid that they've lasted days, weeks, and sometimes months, but my lows could and would sneak up and knock me off my square at any given moment. Though difficult to admit, these extreme ups and downs were a consequence of me avoiding self-care. A type of self-sabotage that cuts deeply. Believing that I had to give myself away to be accepted has been a theme throughout my life. In the community and in business, this self-sacrifice has served me well. In my being, however, living selflessly has often rerouted me to anxiety-ridden days and depression-filled nights. It was the last time, though, three years, almost to the day of the global pandemic-induced shutdown, that finally brought me back to the world with clarity and direction like never before. The moment of truth, if you will.

THAT ONE TIME, AT BAND CAMP

It had been days since I'd had a shower—and weeks since I'd ventured outside of the perimeter of my home's haven. Ignoring calls and missing meetings had become the norm and felt like habits that I was never destined to break. I'd had two visitors– friends who were concerned by my absence in the community. They were refreshing reminders of the world that still existed just beyond my gates, yet the visits left me emptier than before. These days, I can attribute that amplified emptiness to Imposter Syndrome. Hearing my visitors talk about all of the reasons I had to be grateful, proud, and acknowledge my power and place in the world were overwhelming examples of why I had to keep up appearances. So many had been looking to me, learning from me, following me. The well-intended takeaways as I saw them were "Dust yourself off and try again" and "This too, shall pass". In hindsight, they were right. When sitting in it, the words just broke me down more. I could feel the weight growing more forcibly on my shoulders, and all I wanted to do was shrink. After all, my weakness was showing, and this, for me, was not the behavior of a leader. I felt more like a desolate soul ready to throw in the towel.

After vowing to take no more callers, I made a call of my own. Through tears, I petitioned for a house call from my therapist, and without hesitation, she obliged. "This morning," I began to recount, "I woke up and wished I hadn't." She was concerned, I could tell. But she met the revelation with patience, logic, and therapeutic competency. By the end of the house call, I felt much more human, much more in touch with my emotions, and so clear about the direction I had to take. As I replayed our interaction in my mind, I began to obsessively search for an in-patient treatment program that could address my manic-depressive disorder and help me learn to cope with the diagnosis that I had received some twenty years prior. After a few denials, a quick stint in a Texas facility, and some redirection, I found a bed at a center in my home state of Utah. It is here where I would come in touch with my own feelings and address my needs for the first time in adulthood.

It's where I would have my most recent watershed moment. The moment that has brought me together with you right now, doing the thing that I'm purposed to do—share and connect to help those in search of strength to overcome.

ARE YOU SMARTER THAN A FIFTH GRADER?

One thing is for certain: we don't know what we don't know. And collectively, we don't know how to manage our emotions. In school, we learn social interaction on a surface level. "Be kind. Be nice. Behave." These directives speak nothing of interacting with others or, more importantly, interacting with oneself. I didn't know that the pain of depression that I suffered through regularly could be regulated through self-realization, therapy, and, for me, medication. I'd tried therapy and medication individually and collectively, but the effects never lasted more than a spell. I didn't know that the magic ingredient could only be found within.

Amid my treatment, I underwent a profound realization: I had never been taught how to effectively communicate with myself or with others. It struck me that despite the myriad tools available for human interaction and self-reflection, I had never received the guidance to employ them. This epiphany was a turning point, for it led me to acknowledge that my journey toward healing would require a fundamental shift in my approach to self-care and interpersonal connection. Embracing this newfound awareness, I committed to leaning into change, recognizing that doing so was the first crucial step toward my healing process. By opening myself up to this transformative journey, I began to prioritize self-care, understanding that nurturing my own well-being was not indulgent but essential. It became clear to me that authentic healing necessitated a willingness to be vulnerable, even with strangers. Stripping away the mask of "The Nikki Walker" that I wore as a shield in my everyday life was both terrifying and liberating.

In sharing my struggles and fears with those around me, I discovered a profound sense of freedom and a deeper connection to my true self. The importance of delving within and undertaking the demanding work of self-awakening became increasingly evident to me. I realized that true healing and personal growth could only be achieved through a commitment to self-discovery and introspection. Learning to navigate the depths of my own emotions and experiences was an essential part of this process, ultimately leading to a greater sense of self-awareness and authenticity. My journey through treatment illuminated the crucial need for learning to communicate with ourselves and others, as well as the transformative power of embracing vulnerability and self-care. It underscored the significance of introspection and self-discovery in the pursuit of genuine awareness and personal evolution.

GOOD GRIEF, CHARLIE BROWN!

While wading through waves of emotion one day at a time, I came upon a formidable opponent in the form of grief. Grief casts a formidable shadow. It blankets the soul with what feels like the weight of the world, and desires to keep you in the dark. But the secret way grief sneaks into the crevices of one's life makes it so sinister. It connects people, places, and things to core memories, asks you to look for your fault in devastating losses, and insists upon being tended to in its designated moments without consideration. Grief had been the monster in the closet that I didn't want to face. From the devastating loss of my first child to the passing of my grandparents and father to the crushing loss of friends, family, and loved ones during the pandemic, I had fought increasingly hard to avoid my nemesis. "Push down and press on" was my internal dialog. And I followed that voice blindly, hoping against all I knew that avoiding the pain would make it go away. But it doesn't go away. Pain deposits on the soul like sugar on a decaying tooth. It rots from the inside out and changes the core of a person's being. I thought for so long that grief only related to the death of loved ones. I learned that we grieve for so much more: relationships, jobs, opportunities, deferred dreams. Much like any bully, though, once confronted grief loses a lot of its bark. By embracing grief, I've been able to unravel so many complicated feelings that I used to carry. I've gained so much freedom in the process of confronting, embracing, and letting go.

To say that every adult should have the opportunity to experience the transformational power of mental health treatment, coaching, and education is an understatement. In a world where so much is put upon each one of us, a mandatory 30-day course in mental health should be afforded to all for the benefit of all. Unfortunately, that, too is a dream likely to be deferred. The practicality isn't there, I know. But even if we look at standard mental health care, people who look like me are grossly underserved and overlooked.

I'm no expert, but according to the National Alliance on Mental Illness (NAMI), Black adults in the United States are more likely than white adults to report persistent symptoms of emotional distress, yet they are less likely to receive adequate care. When we focus specifically on Black women, the disparities become even more pronounced. Studies have found that Black women are more likely to experience feelings of sadness, hopelessness, and worthlessness compared to their white counterparts. I can only speak for myself when I say that these feelings are powerful. They can send one into a downward spiral with no end in sight. That's where I was, in a seemingly lonely and dark inner world where the chances of escape seemed to only exist through drastic and final measures. This is the danger of the shame of mental health treatment. When feelings like worthlessness enter the conversation, it brings shame and paralysis that further infects the wound. Recognizing that seeking professional help is courageous rather than shameful opens doors to treatment that pride would otherwise close.

COURAGE OVER CRISIS

Amid my mental health crisis, I found myself engulfed by a whirlwind of emotions that seemed to threaten my very existence. It was a dark and daunting period that forced me to confront aspects of myself that I had long neglected. Grief, fear, anger, and depression became unwelcome but persistent companions, casting long shadows over my days and nights. In the depths of my despair, I struggled to find my voice, to articulate the storm that raged within me.

However, it was during this harrowing time that I experienced a profound transformation. Faced with no other option, I began communicating with newfound clarity and vulnerability. I discovered that by sharing my innermost thoughts and feelings, I could forge connections with others that transcended the isolating grip of mental illness. Through open and honest dialogue, I began to understand the power of effective communication as a tool for healing and connection. As I reached out for support, I discovered a network of understanding and compassion that I had not known existed, and I realized that I was not alone in my struggles.

Amidst the chaos, I also found the courage to embrace my emotions —the raw, unvarnished truths of my grief, fear, anger, and depression. I allowed myself to sit with these emotions, to acknowledge their presence, and to release the burden of carrying them in isolation. In doing so, I unearthed a reservoir of strength and resilience lying dormant within me. It was a revelation that empowered me to confront the complexities of my inner landscape with newfound courage and self-compassion.

As I navigated the labyrinth of my own healing, I recognized the transformative potential of sharing my experiences with others. I came to understand that my story could serve as a guiding light for those who felt lost in the throes of their own mental health challenges. By openly discussing my battles, I sought to dismantle the stigma surrounding mental illness and to offer a beacon of hope to those who were struggling in silence. I felt a deep sense of purpose in extending a hand of empathy and understanding to those who felt they were drowning in their own despair.

My journey has taught me the immense value of seeking help and support. I have discovered that there is strength in vulnerability and that reaching out for assistance is an act of courage, not weakness. I stand as a testament that it is possible to emerge from the darkest of times and find a renewed sense of purpose and joy. I am committed to encouraging others to confront their mental health issues and to seek the assistance they need and deserve.

To anyone grappling with their mental well-being, I offer these words: you are not alone, and there is hope to be found in the journey toward healing. I urge you to reach out, to speak up, and to take the brave step of seeking help. There is a community of support waiting to embrace you, and there is a brighter future ahead. You deserve to live a life that is not defined by the constraints of mental illness, and I implore you to take the first steps toward reclaiming your well-being. The realization that I needed and *deserved* help was my watershed moment. Waves of change have revived my mind and rejuvenated my desire to walk in my purpose and focus on the work of self-improvement, self-care, and self-awareness so that those I serve in the community have access to my most authentic and effective levels of self.

Remember, folks, your story is not over, and there is a chorus of voices waiting to join you in the symphony of healing and resilience.

ABOUT THE AUTHOR

With over two decades of experience, Nikki's career in public relations has seen her ascend from an associate to a Vice President. An entrepreneur at heart, she launched and successfully ran her own PR firm for a decade, leaving an indelible mark on the industry. Her strategic acumen also shone as the PR director for a national ethnic hair care brand.

In 2017, Nikki's talents attracted the attention of a multibillion-dollar wellness brand in Utah, propelling her to the role of Director of Global Brand Awareness. Her tenure was marked by significant achievements, contributing to the brand's global expansion and impact.

Venturing into the tech space, Nikki now serves as the Director of Community Engagement at a prominent tech company. Here, she dedicates herself to fostering connections and championing diversity and inclusivity within the organization.

Community Commitment:

Nikki extends her impact beyond the boardroom, actively serving on nonprofit boards across Utah. Her involvement with organizations such as the State Workforce Development Board, Utah Foster Care, The Children's Center, The Road Home, and The Utah Black Chamber of Commerce, showcases her commitment to empowering others and creating opportunities for growth.

Accolades and Recognition:

Nikki's contributions have earned her well-deserved recognition. Named one of Utah Business Magazine's 30 Women to Watch, honored by the W Collective's 40 Over 40, and a recipient of the prestigious Stevie Award in 2022, Nikki stands as a symbol of exceptional achievements. Her impact in the technology sector was further acknowledged with the 2021 Women Tech Change Catalyst Award.

www.nikkiwalker.media

12

NAYSHONDRA MERCER, CPC, ELI-MP

I AM: SEEKING MYSELF

Brené Brown opens *The Gifts of Imperfection* by stating that "practicing courage, compassion, and connection in our daily lives is how we cultivate worthiness." She quotes Mary Daly, a theologian, who writes that you become courageous by practicing: "It's like you learn to swim by swimming," says Daly. " You learn courage by couraging".[1]

I couldn't agree more.

I grew up to be the kind of person who practices these concepts daily. I typically do this by "jumping into the deep end" of life's metaphorical swimming pool, where I can practice what it means to act in courageous ways. I have found power in using my voice and speaking up for those who might have lost theirs, and I have found that in doing so, my voice can solve more problems than it creates by staying silent.

But what about those times when you're too afraid to speak up? How can you act in a courageous way when you're so scared?

Being courageous means doing it scared. It is engaging in acts that challenge you. It's in asking them out on a date, for the promotion you deserve, or the romance lacking in your relationship. It is at these moments where your opportunities to practice courage lie. When we act in courage, it means we are "speaking honestly and openly about who we are, about what we're feeling, and about our experiences (good and bad)" (Brown, p.20). By doing so, we are growing our capacity for compassion, supporting the energy that binds us together and helps us not feel so alone.

But to do this, we have to share. I'll go first.

Mine is a story of the scariest day of my life.

It was the day that I was committed to the psychiatric hospital.

EXERCISING COURAGE

I was taxed - mentally and emotionally. I was overwhelmed by constantly trying to people-please in my platonic and romantic relationships and at work. I was newly engaged and looking forward to marriage, but things weren't going well. We were participating in pre-marital counseling and struggling greatly with communication and boundaries. I felt like I couldn't bring a healthy complaint without my partner becoming defensive. However, from their perspective, my approach was too harsh and critical when I addressed a complaint within the relationship. We weren't on the same page, and turning the page was challenging. We could barely disagree without it turning into an argument, and each argument seemed to get worse and worse.

On top of my issues at home with my fiancé, I had significant problems in my relationships with friends and family. I had become a sounding board for my family and would spend hours listening to their concerns, leaving me feeling lonely when I noticed they would only call when they had a problem. I became emotionally attached to their situations and felt responsible for doing my part not to contribute. I wouldn't speak up about how they were showing up in the relationship with me, creating a situation where the people around me could feel comfortable in my uncomfortableness.

Instead of showing myself compassion by exercising healthy boundaries and saying, "Hey, no, I can't today, but I'd be happy to help you when I return from vacation." or "Hey, babe? It hurts my feelings when you talk about me behind my back. Could you talk to me the next time you have a question?" I would fall into the people-pleasing trap and say nothing to self-protect or say yes to everything just to keep the peace.

But I didn't have peace. I felt unheard and like I had lost my voice. I'd ask myself, "How did we get here?" "I thought we healed from all of this shit! How did we get here?!"

This feeling of confusion led to the overthinking and insomnia that would last for months. My insomnia would become so critical that it ultimately triggered a mental breakdown.

I wish I could tell you I remember how it happened, but I don't. Have you ever woken up from a dream that did not feel like a dream and couldn't remember where you were? Or maybe you've had surgery or were put under anesthesia, but when you woke up, you were talking crazy or woke up in a daze?

That was how I felt, except the dazed feeling lasted over a week. The day that I was committed, I was home alone and floating about in that dazed feeling. I felt asleep, dreaming even, but I knew I was awake and something was wrong.

I knew that I needed help, but I was all alone. Or so I thought.

I remembered the friendly leasing professionals in my community and walked to the leasing office to ask someone to help me. Dressed outrageously in layers and layers of sweaters and bathrobes, as it was the end of November and I was cold, I walked to the leasing office and asked to speak with the Community Manager there. As I waited for her to arrive, I began to feel weak and on the verge of passing out. I was floating in and out of consciousness, and everything began to grow dark around me.

Thankfully, the leasing office responded quickly and called an ambulance to take me to the hospital. The Community Manager was committed to my care. She followed the ambulance to the hospital and stayed with me in my hospital room until my fiancé (who was at work) and my family were able to drive in from South Carolina.

The next few days were a blur, and I do not remember how many days to be exact. But I can tell you about the two weeks I was inside and what I learned as a result.

I learned there are spaces where no one is coming to save you. If you're fighting a battle of the mind, my friend, I'm sorry to tell you, but NO ONE is coming to save you.

As a Believer, I felt like Joseph the Dreamer when his brothers ambushed him and threw him into the pit. I began to think about how he must have felt, all alone in his hell, not knowing who or what was next for him.

At least, that was how I felt - my chest, heavy with sorrow and in so much pain it felt like an elephant was sitting on top of my bosom that it hurt to breathe. I was all alone, lying in my hospital bed, weeping. Some days, I'd only leave the bed to eat or use the restroom. Others, I would only move as much as necessary to allow the nurses to take my blood for the fifty-eleventh time. I was tired of being poked and prodded. My arm was bruised from the amount of blood draws I received, and my body was breaking out in a rash from all of the medications they were trying on me. I was stuck. I was too distraught and broken to leave the room or take the phone calls that kept flying in from my family, friends, and co-workers. Even in their worry about me, they still needed and wanted me to show up for them, to give them news or answers about what I was experiencing while on the inside. But what do you say to people when people aren't the answer to your problem? What do you say to the people who contributed to you being in the pit?

You do what Joseph did. You work in service to others until your purpose finds you.

FOSTERING CONNECTION

Joseph would eventually leave the pit and was sold into slavery. It's important to note here that Joseph, to date, is innocent. He hasn't done anything except share his dream with those who could not receive him. Doing so landed him in a pit, then sold into slavery and sent to work for Potipher, who would later enslave Joseph in the King's prison for being unjustly accused of trying to sleep with Potipher's wife.

While in prison, Joseph experiences another pit, except this time, other people are there with him. Most importantly, we also learn that "the Lord was with him; he showed him kindness and granted him favor in the eyes of the prison warden. So the warden put Joseph in charge of all those held in prison and was made responsible for all that was done there. The warden paid no attention to anything under Joseph's care because the Lord was with Joseph and gave him success in whatever he did."[2]

The Lord was with him. And because I have the faith of a mustard seed, I knew God was with me, too. So, on the days when I felt too broken to get up or when I was feeling like a failure for getting so mentally ill that I required hospital treatment, I remembered Joseph and how he dug deep to find his purpose while experiencing the pit. I call this the "dig-deep button."

The "dig-deep" button is "the button that you rely on when you're too bone-tired to get up one more time in the middle of the night or to do one more load of throw-up-diarrhea laundry or catch one more plane or to return one more call or to please/perform/perfect the way you normally do even when you just want to flip someone off and hide under the covers" (Brown 2020, 6).

I was hiding under the covers.

Literally.

When you lose your mind, the whole world feels scary, even when the world is only the four walls of the hospital unit. The hospital was my pit, and I felt stuck. I couldn't leave because I was involuntarily committed, and although I desperately wanted to leave the pit, I was being held against my will - but for my good.

Tell me, friend - what do you do when it is decided that you are not well enough to make decisions for yourself? To determine what you want or don't want, what to eat, what to wear, or even when you bathe.

What do you do?

I didn't know what else to do, so I began to "dig deep." To do this, I deliberated my thoughts and behaviors through prayer, meditation, or simply setting my intentions. I typically fall onto the Serenity Prayer when I'm feeling overwhelmed. It helps to remind me who is in control. Then, I got inspired to make new and different choices. I make a realistic plan to reach my goal. I set myself up for success by contemplating what I **could** do instead of focusing on anything I could not. And finally, I got going by taking action.

After spending too many days hiding under the covers and feeling lonely with a chest full of sadness, I had an energy shift that let me know I had to do something. So what did I do? I deliberated and started making a plan to feel better. I started small by doing the basics: brushing my teeth, showering, getting dressed, and making my bed. After a few days, I felt well enough to be social. I continued to dig deep in the coming days and began to spark conversations with other patients, playing card games with some and practicing yoga with others.

Despite the circumstances that brought us there, one thing was apparent: we all need connection. Human connection is "the energy between people when they feel seen, heard, and valued; when they can give and receive without judgment; and when they derive sustenance and strength from the relationship" (Brown 2020, 29). While navigating our journeys of getting well and being discharged from the hospital, we shared this experience.

Sharing an experience with another and building a connection with them also reminded me of Joseph's story. I remembered the part of the story when Joseph attempted to foster relationships with the Cupbearer and the Baker while in the King's prison. In the story, we learn that some time passed after Joseph was imprisoned by Potipher when the Cupbearer and the Baker offended their master, the Pharaoh. Pharaoh was said to have been so angry and put his men in the custody of the guard's captain in the same prison where Joseph was confined. The captain of the guard assigned them to Joseph, and he attended to them when, one day, Joseph noticed the Cupbearer and the Baker in distress and asked them what the matter was (Gen 40: 1-7).

This part of the story reminds me of the day I heard a fellow patient in distress and offered my services to help.

Several days had passed since my intake to the hospital, and I was beginning to feel better and motivated towards being discharged. I had just finished lunch and was walking back to my room when I noticed a patient in tears while talking on the phone with her family. She was upset about her appearance, precisely, her hair.

I felt that.

I felt her sadness in my chest first and then my throat. It was full of unshed tears that I was holding back as I watched her cry and plead with her loved one on the other end of the phone in her attempt to get some understanding and compassion.

Just like me, the young lady had natural, coily hair. Although the hospital products were not the most top-rated for Black hair, I managed to get by using a few squirts of a Taraji P. Henson product that I had to practically break my neck for as another patient exited the hospital and gave it away. Despite the circumstances, I couldn't help but notice the lack of attention to such details as shampoo and conditioner for hair types like mine. Of course, the hospital's purpose was to stabilize their patients' minds and get us back home with our loved ones, but this stood out to me.

The young lady grew more and more upset. She was on the verge of yelling and began to cry harder, declaring, "You don't understand!"

But I understood.

I understood what it felt like to be in a place where you don't belong, and everything around you, even the simple choice of shampoo and conditioner to use, silently tells you that you do not belong there. This feeling, understanding, and energy shift led me to make the connection and what I did next.

I walked up behind her on the phone and said, "Hey, baby girl. Would you like me to help you with your hair?"

With tears in her eyes, she nodded "yes" and gave me a weak smile.

I would spend the next four hours styling and twisting her hair into cute mini twists. As I styled, I felt her energy shift. She was long away from the tears and desperation that she was in just hours before. Instead, she appeared happy and was very grateful once it was complete.

I would see her in the following days and notice how much more confidence she exuded. When she smiled, I could hear India Arie's song, "I Am Not My Hair," playing in my ears. While she was certainly **not** her hair, the simple act and connection fostered in her hair's styling is the energy that makes one feel seen, heard, and valued. I realized that even in the darkest places, in the lowest of pits, you can pull yourself out by seeking connection with others.

GROWING COMPASSION - TENDING TO WHO YOU ARE BECOMING

The day finally came when I almost broke into a dance while leaving the hospital. Thank God! After two long weeks, I finally made it out of the pit! Now was my chance to live it up and share my gifts with the world.

I felt like Joseph when he interviewed for a job with Pharaoh.

The story picks up with the Cupbearer and the Baker having their dreams interpreted by Joseph, and all his predictions come true. "Now, the third day was Pharaoh's birthday, and he gave a feast for all his officials. Pharaoh lifted the heads of the chief cupbearer and the chief baker in the presence of his officials: He restored the chief cupbearer to his position so that he once again put the cup into Pharaoh's hand - but he impaled the chief baker, just as Joseph had said to them in his interpretation. The chief Cupbearer, however, did not remember Joseph; he forgot him" (Gen 40: 20-23).

Have you ever been in a place where you were expecting someone else to deliver on something that you previously did for them, but they didn't do it? It's like you're holding your breath, waiting for their permission to breathe again - but they never do and suddenly you're choking. I suspect that's how Joseph felt after he assisted the Cupbearer.

By now, we have learned that Joseph is patient, and we see that he will later get another opportunity to make his gifts known to Pharaoh. His chance comes when Pharaoh has two troubling dreams that none of Egypt's magicians or wise men could interpret. "Pharaoh told them his dreams, but no one could interpret them for him" (Gen 41:8).

Here was Joseph's opportunity, and he was ready. After spending years behind the scenes working in service to others, from working diligently in Potiphar's house to serving the Baker and Cupbearer while still imprisoned, Joseph never acted like he was the victim of his circumstances. Instead, he preserves by sharing his gifts with others and making a connection. Joseph shows himself and others compassion through his care and understanding of their needs and concerns.

"Pharaoh told Joseph, 'I had a dream, and no one can interpret it. But I have heard it said of you that when you hear a dream, you can solve it.

'I cannot do it,' Joseph replied to Pharaoh, 'but God will give Pharaoh the answer he desires'" (Gen 41:15-16).

Much like Joseph, when I was in my hospital pit and acting in service to others, I did not believe that there was anything that I could do to help those around me.

"I cannot do it," I'd say to myself repeatedly. "I cannot do it." But this way of thinking wasn't helping me to climb out of the pit, so I dug deep and landed on another thought.

"Maybe I can't do it. Maybe I can't change anything or anyone. But God can."

And with this new energy and shift, I re-entered the world on a mission to share my gifts.

What does it mean to share one's gifts with the world?

Good question. The answer is simple - the answers are all within you. God can use you and the gifts he gave you to empower others to do what we are all on Earth to do: heal our hearts and save ourselves from unnecessary suffering by accessing the power invested in us. A power that comes from above. When we do this, we accept our reality as humans with limited control over most of life's uncomfortable moments, like breaking up with a partner, getting laid off from a job, losing a child, or even receiving a diagnosis that will rock your world.

I left the hospital with a diagnosis that would rock most people's worlds.

Like Edgar Allen Poe, Van Gogh, Britney Spears, and Mariah Carey, I am in the small 6% of the world who live with and navigate through Bipolar Disorder. However, despite what the world would have me believe, this diagnosis did not rock my world. No - in fact, it did the exact opposite. It empowered me and allowed me to advocate for others in the world and the workplace simply by being myself and honoring where I am at any moment, even if it makes me or others uncomfortable.

I learned that when we lean into our uncomfortable moments and learn to navigate through the pits of our hell, we make room for more understanding and compassion for ourselves and others. When we practice courage and share our stories honestly and openly about who we are and what we have experienced, we create the space for others to do the same, contributing to the collective and the mass awakenings of nations through awareness.

This is my story of learning, growth, and empowerment that became the awareness that put me on.

ABOUT THE AUTHOR

Nayshondra Mercer brings over a decade of expertise in behavioral modification, learning and development, organizational change management, and strategic planning. Born in Wuerzburg, Germany to two army soldiers, Nayshondra gained worldly experience from a young age through travel and connections. She spent most of her childhood in her hometown of Columbia, South Carolina, where she first developed her passion for learning. Nayshondra quickly discovered that her path to making a difference in the world was through continuous learning and personal growth.

While pursuing her Bachelor of Arts in Political Science and African American Studies at Winthrop University, Nayshondra embarked on a career in Social Work, serving as a public servant for children and families in the foster care system for over a decade. Nayshondra also earned her M.A. in Political Science and Public Policy from American Military University. She has expanded her expertise by obtaining certifications in training from the University of South Carolina and two coaching certifications from the Institute of Professional Excellence in Coaching (iPEC). In 2021, she established her coaching practice, Crossing Bridges Coaching, LLC.

Currently residing in Atlanta, GA, Nayshondra is embarking on a new journey in Multifamily Property Management. Her mission remains focused on shaping futures through knowledge and empowerment!

www.nayshondramercer.com

13

DAVID C. ATKINS

NAVIGATING THE CROSSROADS OF LIFE

This chapter is dedicated to my mother, Daisy B. Atkins, my greatest source of inspiration.

NEGOTIATING INTERNAL CONFLICT

At the age of thirty-eight, I experienced the most significant death in my lifetime, that of my mother. While my father died when I was just ten years of age, my maternal grandfather at fifteen, and my maternal grandmother at thirty-three, the death of my mother resonated at my core. Perhaps this is because I was the youngest of five siblings and I had the opportunity to live alone with her for about three years after all my siblings had left the nest. This time allowed me to build a special bond with my mother as I received her non-competitive attention. I learned so many things from her, including financial and business management. She was a business owner and I watched her for years manage Daisy's Beauty Salon and account for revenue. Her value of excellence truly lives within me.

My mother's death signified to me that I was now able to solely provide for myself without any assistance from her or others. When

I left for college in 1985, I recall packing everything, making several trips to place things in the car, and noticing my mother sitting on her bed looking out the window silently crying. Before I left for my trip to Northern Virginia, my mother said to me in her parting words, "I will not die before you are able to take care of yourself." At that moment, I didn't give much thought to what she had said. But this declaration stayed with me, planted in the inner core of my being. So, I found myself avoiding the inevitable by either intentionally or subconsciously creating situations throughout my life to demonstrate that I wasn't quite able to take care of myself. One day in my early thirties, I called my mother to share with her the negative results and fall-out of a financial investment at which time in the midst of listening and comforting me, I heard her say, "I thought you were my guy." It was the voice of disappointment in which my response was silence. As an adult, I had not experienced that feeling from my mother. I felt lost and alone, and wasn't quite sure how to navigate her early sentiment of "I will not die before you are able to take care of yourself" and "I thought you were my guy." I am certain my mother didn't realize the psychological reconciliation I had to make with those two contradictory sentiments. The internal struggle of me living my life without major challenges so she would be proud of me, while at the same time ensuring she would be here with me to enjoy life was a balancing-act I was always trying to achieve.

When my mother began her second battle with cancer, I started to demonstrate to her that I was okay, that she had done well by me, and that I could live fully independently. My mother was highly independent, and I recall having to physically support her during a visit home with a very personal matter and thinking this alone would cause my mother to choose death. Later, we were all sitting in the family room and my mother and I were facing the

Daisy B. Atkins

large pane window with the draperies drawn open allowing us to see outside. My mother began to look intently out the window as if a visitor had driven up the driveway and started saying, "They are coming, they are coming." I took a more cautious look through that window and clearly noticed that no one was outside. I didn't question my mother or give her any doubt about what she was seeing, as it appeared to me that she was having a moment of spiritual transcendence. She was acknowledging verbally that her transition was actively being prepared for her. It was one of the greatest spiritual moments I had ever witnessed since my own personal experiences of touches by the Holy Spirit.

My mother died within two weeks of her moment of spiritual transcendence. I was devastated. My mother's words of, "I will not die before you are able to take care of yourself," resonated even more strongly with me as I was now living in that moment. Not only had she transitioned, but so had I. I had transitioned to a place of full human independence. It was new territory but I was determined to conquer it, perhaps sometimes at levels of over-compensation, as my way to honor my mother's words. Thus, my strength was, and often still is, an over-compensation to live up to the declaration made by my mother. And now ensuring that I never hear the disappointing echo of "I thought you were my guy."

We all have life experiences that shape how we move, think, and engage throughout this world and with others. It is upon us as living vessels to draw upon those experiences and navigate this thing we call life here on Earth the best we can. There is no perfect recipe, solution, or way to live life. However, if we can find that motivation that requires us to be well, to do good, to strive for our best, our lives will be more fulfilled and purposeful, and perhaps keep us more grounded and mentally well.

THE CARRYOVER IN THE WORKPLACE

After my mother's burial, I returned to work fairly quickly to keep my mind busy and focus on positive things. I worked at a university and was very engaged with many students and their work and organizational activities. My office was in one of the largest campus facilities with four levels with open atrium architecture. You are probably thinking now, why is this detail so important? Well, let me tell you. On my first day back at work, I walked by the tallest atrium architecture which allows you to look from the highest floor to the ground floor. I had simply grabbed a cup of coffee and was returning to my office. Within minutes of passing that architecture, a student jumped from it to his death. It was reported and shared with me that the facility's video cameras showed me walking by the student who jumped within minutes of me passing him.

How could it be possible that after burying my mother, I returned to work to experience the suicide of a student? I remember my supervisor coming to my office to see how I was doing. I shared that I feel like there is a hole inside of my body. The hole was there due to the loss of my mother, but somehow it felt even larger after learning a student jumped to his death moments after walking by him. What if I had just slowed down a bit, paid a little more attention to my surroundings? Would I have noticed this student and been able to offer an alternative voice for him? Could I have prevented his death that day only if I had seen him? I believe I was placed near that student for an intended purpose but failed to slow down and listen to the greater voice. I prayed over that student and his family for weeks in my attempt to reconcile my feelings of loss and failure.

These back-to-back encounters with death helped shape how I saw people and things. How did I ever allow the political climate of a workplace overshadow my innate desires to care for others? In the past when I had seen students sit alone on the floor or against a wall, seemingly hurt or upset, I would quietly sit next to them to simply check on them and offer some words of encouragement if needed. How did this moment pass me by? Was it the workplace environment causing a distraction or was it that I was still in the process of mourning? But I was placed there for a purpose! I failed.

I heard the echo of "I thought you were my guy." So soon after burying my mother, I heard her voice of disappointment.

People who have closely worked with me in the church, my fraternity, and professionally recognize my unique leadership style. I am a visionary, yet very detailed and specific, which is often found challenging by those I lead. Our experiences shape us and inform how we will navigate society. I cannot fail. And if I do, it is highly likely no one will ever know as my level of excellence is so high my failure is not noticed. Thus, I am protected from the echo of disappointment.

JOURNEY THROUGH WELLBEING

As humans, we experience internal conflict throughout our lives. They could include the fear of failure, the tussle between good and evil, or the wrestling with one's own destiny. My primary internal conflict is the fear of failure. In the past, I have always associated failure as a barrier to success, while in later life, I have learned that failure often translates to success. What would you consider to be your primary internal conflict? How have you managed this conflict to be able to lead effectively? My fear of failure had me so focused on metrics and outcomes that I lost my sight of the care for other people. There are a few things that I do and highly recommend as techniques to help manage internal conflict that might assist in stronger and healthy leadership.

1. Be aware of your internal conflict and stop, sit down, and relax. Take a few deep breaths, think about where you are and your surroundings. Then, speak out loud, for you to hear, three to five positive things you saw, heard, or thought about in that moment. This should assist you in calming your spirit.
2. Call a friend. Reach out to someone you trust and who understands you to attempt to seek perspective. Talking and listening to them helps alleviate some of the mental clutter.

3. Get physical. Walk at a fast pace or do some light running with the goal of elevating your heart rate. This changes the chemical messaging to your brain and allows you to calm down.

I have found using these techniques helps keep me grounded, and focused on the important thing in life – people, and tunes out all of the negative forces and voices.

UNEXPECTED TURNS

Many life experiences have increased my awareness whereby they served as a catalyst for change. In this chapter, I specifically focused on two deaths – one in my personal life and the other in the workplace. Other experiences include my ministry education and calling, my fraternity life, my professional and workplace encounters, my volunteer involvement, my foster parenting engagement, and my international travel excursions. While all of these experiences contributed to life-changing moments for me, it was my international travel adventures that altered my perspective on life experiences in America and the world. In 2018, I had the opportunity to join a group of adult travelers from multiple states and countries on a travel adventure to Egypt. This was my very first international trip as an adult. I took every precaution possible and purchased travel insurance, medical insurance, and terrorist attack insurance. I didn't drink the water or eat fruit washed. For thirteen days I lived out of a carry-on suitcase as I feared losing my luggage or having it stolen, which happened to some travelers. I met some of the most wonderful people on the trip, including the Egyptians.

The residents of Egypt appeared to be mostly poor in the places that we visited. Some residents used their homes as museums so tourists could see what life was like in residential communities as a way to generate income. In one home we visited, they offered drinks, snacks, and henna tattoos. Visiting the residents' homes was one of my most favorite parts of the excursion. To see how the homes were structured and decorated was extremely fascinating to me. I loved engaging with the locals in Egypt. I loved learning about their political system, a dictatorship, and how many felt about their president who had been in office since 2014. I found most were not very comfortable with my questions as it was not deemed popular to speak against him as I learned from our tour guide.

I remember being part of a segment of travelers who ventured off from our security, at least so we thought, to really immerse ourselves in the culture. We explored the local market in Aswan, Egypt to learn during our return to the riverboat on the Nile, where we stayed most of the trip, that we were being followed by our security when some from the group needed assistance crossing the road. As we were feeling the desire to be "amongst the people" in a social setting, we asked our tour guide to take us to a local bar for drinks and hookah. Later that evening we went to a local bar where we sat at a table on the street and just absorbed the atmosphere of the community. This was my first-time smoking hookah, which was a very common thing in Egypt. I can't think of a better place to experience hookah for the first time. Yes, it was awesome! Everything about it was just awesome! The people were welcoming, engaging, and some even curious about America and asked us questions to get a sense of what it was like to live in America.

During my time in Egypt, I allowed myself to operate outside my comfort zone in so many aspects of this trip that I surprised myself. I engaged more openly with the folks in whom I was traveling and developed relationships with some beyond the trip. I ate food that perhaps I would not have normally and found most of it enjoyable. I adapted to traditional customs to demonstrate my respect for their traditions such as removing shoes when entering the mosques in Cairo, Egypt. I also witnessed theft, a child run over by a car, and attempted theft of my identity and wallet. This alone was a lot in just thirteen days! We actually had to have a tour guide replaced as he was converting currency for some of the travelers when one of them realized that they were not receiving the correct amount back in the Egyptian pound. The bank was providing the accurate exchange amount but he was pocketing a portion of it before he delivered the funds to the traveler.

While visiting Cairo, Egypt we were taken to a location to take picturesque photos with the pyramids. It was here where I climbed a large rock with this young lady to take my photo with the pyramid in the background. I became comfortable with her as she suggested that I place my passport, which was around my neck with other I.D., cash, and credit cards, on the ground. So, I did! Of course, the photos would look better without this passport holder dangling from my neck, right? At some point, my inner spirit said to look over my shoulder. I saw a man slowly approaching me. Now there were three people on this large rock. I reached down and picked up my passport holder, and placed it back around my neck. The photo shoot quickly came to an end.

The Pyramids of Egypt, taken by David C. Atkins

While the level of alertness required was a little exhausting, I gained an unprecedented appreciation of the culture of people in Egypt that I may not have ever been able to grasp without visiting the country. Developing relationships with travelers from America who were actually born in Africa proved to be rewarding as well. These relationships afforded me even more personal knowledge about another culture of people and inspired me to visit Ghana just months after returning from Egypt. I love learning about different cultures and people. It's the absolute best! Have you considered traveling internationally? If not, what is holding you back? I encourage you to do so if you can. You will garner an appreciation for other cultures and a greater appreciation for your own. It will better position you to operate at levels above the nonsense, games, and issues of people in your personal and work lives. It is hard to visit another country and not be changed in some way or begin to think differently. I have found myself, personally, being even more open to people from different cultures and actually engaging in dialogue with them from a place of authenticity to learn about them individually. Disengaging with individuals who do not prove themselves worthy of my energy seems to occur more often now, and my level of tolerance for people in authority who operate from the place of authority and not leadership is significantly lower. The things I once found important or placed some level of value to I no longer share the same sentiments.

THE LAST WORD

I have come to learn that there is never a "last word." We are evolving everyday as humans and what we know to be yesterday, today, and even tomorrow may very well be something different next week, next month, or next year. So, with this understanding, how do we navigate life's intricate journey in a way that capitalizes on personal growth and serves as a conduit that touches the lives of others in a manner that is positive? How do we use our individual and collective experiences and "know-how" to elevate others and thus our communities as a whole?

It has been my mother's words of concern and care stated as, "I will not die before you are able to take care of yourself," coupled with her expression of disappointment shared as "I thought you were my guy," that has kept me on a fairly focused path. They have also helped me maintain my mental health and sense of belonging even in places that work hard at not creating welcoming environments. Strength is found in my mother's words, and my commitment to honor her with excellence and success will never be sacrificed for the benefit of others who don't place people first.

My lived experiences cause me to engage with and trust people in ways that sometimes can be mis-interpreted and maybe even a little challenging for others. I have learned to be an intrusive leader out of concern for others who only trust people who have demonstrated they deserve that gift from me. I often time care for people at levels not widely experienced by many. I genuinely express concern for the wellbeing of those in my circle, and while it is appreciated by some, others don't quite understand how to receive the gift of care. Some even see kindness as a weakness to later learn of the mistake in doing so. Be as open and available to those around you but be earnest in protecting your wellbeing. Show a compassionate spirit and avail yourself of what is happening in the moment. It has made a great difference in how I relate to people and find greater happiness within.

ABOUT THE AUTHOR

David C. Atkins has had an interesting, diverse, and complicated journey while navigating his time here on Earth, primarily as a Virginia resident. Raised in a small town called Jarratt, located in Sussex County, the first school he attended, Jefferson Elementary School, was named in honor of his family, which was founded by his great-great-grandmother. David was ordained as a minister at Chapel Hill Baptist Church which his great-great-grandmother also founded.

David is a founding member of the George Mason University Black Alumni Chapter and longest-serving president of the chapter. He is also a charter member of the Iota Alpha Chapter of Alpha Phi Alpha Fraternity, Inc. at George Mason and an honorary member of the Order of Omega. He holds a Bachelor's degree from George Mason, where he has a 35+ year relationship as student, alumni, employee, donor, and fundraiser. He is currently the Executive Director of Brand Development and Licensing at his alma mater. He also has a Master's degree in Theology from Howard University, where he decided to accept his calling to the ministry.

David's passion lies in inspiring young minds to achieve greatness, a mission that brings him peace. His international travel experiences, especially to Egypt and Ghana, have enriched his perspectives. David is also an avid sports fan of the George Mason Patriots, Dallas Cowboys, and the Golden State Warriors.

14

RAMALL JOHNSON

UNPACKING THE LESSONS FOUND ON THE OTHER SIDE

Life has always been an amazing teacher, even if I have not been the best of students. It is consistent and unrelenting in its approach until I learn the lesson.

Looking back now, I can see those moments and connect the dots to the present. I am the sum of my actions, my thoughts, my words, and more importantly, how I felt about the things that happened to me.

Hindsight is 20/20.

True vision, however, is seeing the connection of the past projected into the future. I want to share a few pivotal points of awareness that have forever shaped my life.

It all began exactly one lifetime ago. Even though I have not lived there in almost 30 years, it is Home. I still see those bright smiles and waving hands as friends and strangers alike greet you as they drive past. Neighbors and family stopped in to say hello and see how everyone was doing. I still feel the joy and pride in my mom Loretta's eyes as I share with her my latest achievements. I can still feel the strong and guiding presence of my grandfather, Carol

Bourgeois, as he taught us about faith and how to kneel and pray. I still feel the warmth of the hugs from my grandmother, Nellie Mae, that always seemed to feel right and melt anything the world could throw at me. Growing up in my hometown of Jeanerette, Louisiana, life was overflowing with these moments.

As I close my eyes, I can still see those tall green stalks of sugarcane rustling as the wind blows. I still smell that sweet, syrupy aroma that wafts through the air as it's released during its processing stages. I can still hear the laughter of children playing. My sister Natasha and older brother Quentin would race our bikes around the dirt track carved into the grass in the backyard by our endless battles. We would play for hours underneath those massive pecan trees that seemed to touch the skies. During the right time of year those same trees would rain down hundreds of tasty pecans. During the spring and early summer, we would lie on our backs staring at the clouds, pointing out things we imagined. "Do you see that dragon?!" "Look at that spaceship!" We would be lost in our own endless world, occasionally brought back to earth by an ant bite or buzzing bee that was a little too curious.

These were the carefree adventure filled days of my youth. My childhood taught me about faith, community, family, and love. This was my origin story.

But there were those other moments, too, where reality stepped in and changed things.

I was the kind of kid that spent time not only with my friends but also connecting with their parents. It always felt like an extended family.

I remember being home for the funeral of the father of close family friends.

I remember talking with the mom of the family, Laura Mae, attempting to offer condolences and solace. In the midst of my feeble words, she stopped me abruptly and asked me one of the most profound questions I had heard: "When you look at a cemetery, what do you see?" I began to describe what I saw, but as I looked at her face, I realized I was not answering her question. In her eyes, I saw a complex mixture of deep and resounding loss and a sense of hope for the future. She gently grabbed my shoulder with a touch of that old-school wisdom.

She said, "I see the cure for cancer, I see the cure for world hunger, I see solutions for world peace. It's all there in the potential of the people who died but didn't fulfill the purpose God had for their life. Don't let the sun go down on your dreams or his purpose in your life."

Such strength and conviction in a moment of unimaginable loss and despair. She was still thoughtful enough to reach through her grief to inspire me and share a message of hope with a young man finding his way. I took away two lessons from her wisdom:

1. Even in my darkest hours, I will have the chance to touch someone's life. In a hurting world, God will give me opportunities to create a life of impact if I extend myself and engage.
2. Being true to myself and clear with my purpose will create doors for me and allow me to do the same for others. I must focus on strengthening my strength. I can grow into the best version of me or a watered-down version of someone else.

These lessons have resonated with me for 31 years. They have guided me to my purpose throughout life. As a child, when asked, "What do you want to be when you grow up?" I never had an answer. "I want to be a pilot. I want to be a doctor. I want to be a firefighter. I want to be a judge." No answer ever felt genuine. I often wondered why. I struggled because my answer was never centered around a "what."

My truth has always centered around "who" I want to be. Self actualization was my superpower. I was keenly aware of what was important, what drove me and my unique approach. It reminded me of a scene from Spiderman when Peter Parker is bit by the radioactive spider and realizes that he no longer needs glasses because he can see clearly. Through my actions, in my thoughts, by way of my words, my True North is that I want to help. I wanted to make a difference for good. I feel alive when I connect with people and help in moments of need.

Throughout my career I have led at some of the most dynamic and innovative companies like Apple, Wells Fargo, and Chase. I have been able to coach, develop, lead, and inspire thousands of people to perform and produce exceptional results. One philosophy has guided me: find a way to help people in need. No matter the company's objective I always lead through this servant leadership focus. It has always yielded amazing results. Within my first year at Apple I led my store to be the number one sales production business team in the entire region. That was done through building connections, understanding their hopes, dreams, and fears, beyond Apple. I sought to serve and truly help them as individuals. This created a synergy that went beyond just company goals. This model has continued throughout my career. That desire to make a positive impact and inspire change was seeded in my youth. It is my compass rose or a lighthouse guiding me to my destination.

There comes a time, however, where life's challenges demand decisive action. There comes a moment when we must stand firm and make a decision, or the relentless drift of life will make the decision for us. It is a crucial opportunity when we must examine our beliefs and can no longer allow our feelings to lead us like a proverbial moth to a flame. This is pivotal. We must take charge and steer the rudder of life. Events in life can thrust us into a state of self-preservation and trigger a primal instinct to avoid pain and harm.

I remember the exact moment. It is crystal clear. It is a beautiful Christmas morning. The air outside is brisk, and the house is decorated with all the holly, lights, and cheer. My eyes are still heavy. The night before, my son and I were putting together a giant trampoline outside for my daughter in 30-degree weather. I can still feel the chill in my bones. It is time to celebrate the birth of our Lord and Savior. Joy to the world, the Lord has come.

The Christmas music is playing softly in the background. The aroma of the amazing breakfast I just prepared still lingers in the air. Excitement, anticipation, and laughter fill the air as my kids prepare to open their gifts. Yet in the midst of this moment, I feel so alone, and the quiet desperation of my soul cries out…. "Save Me."

Like many others the holiday season brings its own melancholy and sadness. It's a reminder of the ones we have lost and those future moments without their presence.

To truly understand you have to go deeper into my history.

I was reared by my grandfather. My biological father and I did not have a relationship. After he and my mom divorced, it was like I lost him as well. I was told that he was incredibly intelligent, handsome, and athletic. He was president of the Men's Student Government Association of his university. He was Dean of Pledges for his fraternity Alpha Phi Alpha. He was just not in my or my sister's life.

I can still remember the year, 1998. It was one of the most challenging of my life. My son, my legacy, was born in July. My grandfather, who raised me, died of cancer the next month. And a few months later, my biological father died. In one year, I became a father, lost the only one I knew, and then lost the one with whom I never got a chance to reconcile. Waves of pain and depression flowed through my soul. In that season, I made a promise to myself to create a family, to be there every night when they went to sleep and every morning when my kids opened their eyes, no matter what. This world has far too often told the lie that black men are not responsible for their kids. I grew up with too many real-life examples to know that was never true. This was not their fate. This is not my destiny.

Growing up I was empowered to change the things in my life that I didn't like. I saw my mom get up early every morning before the sun was out to get us ready for school, then head off to work eight plus grueling hours a day as a seamstress in a Fruit of the Loom factory. She did this to provide a better life for us. My grandfather showed me what it meant to be a man for God, a loving husband, a strong caring father, and a good friend and neighbor. Many days I sat and watched him fix the family car underneath that white metal carport on that gravel driveway. I saw him grab his toolbox with the slightly rusty old hammer with the wooden handle time and again when something broke in the home. I saw him sit and have conversations with my grandmother, figuring out how to pay the bills or help someone who really needed their help.

I also saw Him in those quiet moments. I remember peeking through that old wooden door to the bedroom, trying not to make it creak. And there he was, on his knees praying, asking God for answers, that his will be done. I saw my grandmother, with a strength that still amazes me, work all day as a cook in an elementary school cafeteria and then come home and help anyone in need without hesitation. Even though she was tired, she was selfless in her actions, with a heart filled with love for people.

I had the blueprint for happiness. I saw it every day growing up. Put and keep God first, work hard, and help others.

But there is a storm on the horizon, and I am helpless to do anything against it. The world as I knew it is at its end.

I don't understand this part of my journey. It seems off course. The marriage and family that I prayed for all those years ago seem to fracture before my very eyes and I am powerless.

I ask, I pray, I beg, but God's answer appears to be no. Now it seems that our wills compete. He seems to have other plans. God, "Please, please help me fix this. Show me what you want me to do."

His reply, "What did I already show you?"

And then silence.

Left alone with just my thoughts can be a dangerous place especially when things are not going well or at least the way I planned. The seeds of doubt, fear, and resentment kick in. I can't fix this.

When do I say goodbye to the dream I cultivated in my adolescence of creating a happy loving family unit? The joy and love have been replaced by a deteriorating reality. I can't turn down the noise of my thoughts on replay in my head, the arguing, the heartbreak. I have become comfortable with dysfunction.

It's like wearing an old sock. The fabric is worn from repeated wear. There are holes in the heel and toe areas. The elastic that once fit perfectly around my legs has stretched, and they now droop and flop around my ankles. They are not the same.

I can't just throw them out, though. These are my lucky socks. I remember that time way back when all was right with the world. I could do no wrong. Great things were happening. I was wearing these socks then.

But they are not my lucky socks. They are just a faded memory of what used to be. That feeling of warmth and support I once felt has been replaced. There is frustration now every time my toe sticks through that hole. It's an uncomfortable, dull pain that I have grown accustomed to feeling.

Is this life? The arguments, the stress, the confusion, the deception, the hurt? This can't be love. That vision I had for my life has left me. This is it, though, the final breath of a dream of love that is no more. Do I ignore that feeling that has been eating away inside me? No matter how insanely I wanted it to work and it could be for all the right reasons. If it is wrong, it is not right.

Family is everything to me, so this is by no means a small or easy step. How long have I betrayed my heart and mind holding onto hope for a life I built in my head so many years ago? We have traveled so far past the breaking point. I am a fighter but what do I do with this feeling? I know in my heart without a shadow of a doubt, what I do and do not want. This can not continue. I will not survive this. This caricature I have become to protect my heart and mind has made me unrecognizable to myself. Make my decision and own it. So after my last child graduated I chose peace. I chose healing. I chose me.

The past is something I have no power to change. There is a purpose in the lesson. It is only through my thoughtful and intentional decisions that I create my future. I choose Life beyond the pain. I take action but most importantly, I pray and trust that God will guide my every step. Faith is the only answer.

Pain has been my access point to a deeper understanding of self. My question of introspection has always been, what did I learn from this moment?

This forces me to analyze the situation and understand how I can grow from the experience. It puts me into an action phase. I am responsible for my life and what it holds. I was able to survive through the suffering and figure out the meaning. Holding on to the pain no longer serves its purpose. It is only through the release of the pain that true liberation comes. In this new season, holding onto it would destroy the possibility of a fresh start fueled by a new perspective.

The distance between me and changing my situation is one decision. It may be painful. It may be scary and unknown. I have to be the one to make it. Sometimes I have to let go of an old, faded dream to choose a better future.

It's hard to describe this feeling now. God's warmth, love, and sunshine cover me. There is beauty after the pain. After praying, the self-work, learning to let go and to forgive myself for not being strong enough to make it work. I can breathe again. My vision is clear. The world is new. I no longer feel like myself, which is a strange statement. I shed the old things in me that can not benefit this new version. I am forever becoming who I am meant to be.

To God Be the Glory! Today is always the first day of the rest of life! Don't miss it!

To my amazing kids Daylon and Amyah. I love you from the depths of my soul. My greatest joy is knowing that God trusted me to begin your journey as you change this world for His glory. Boldly run into who you are meant to be.

To that green eyed angel who rescued me.... no one else could have saved me. I am forever in your debt. Tracy I can not wait to see what God will do through us. The world awaits before us.

To my friend the incredibly talented Chantée Christian thank you for the opportunity to share my truth and add to this incredible project!

ABOUT THE AUTHOR

Ramall Johnson is a passionate believer and seasoned professional with over 20 years of leadership excellence. His transformative style, coupled with a visionary approach, positioned him as a valuable asset in multiple Fortune 500 companies ranging from the technical innovation space to the financial services sector.

He has a proven track record of recruiting, developing, and leading successful teams in sales, marketing, and production. With a strong foundation in facilitation, innovative problem resolution, and interpersonal skills, he consistently drives organizational success.

Ramall, a native of Jeanerette, Louisiana, currently resides in Houston, Texas, and is the proud father of a son and daughter.

15

J. ARTEL SMITH

FROM STRUGGLE TO STRENGTH

In a world that often encourages us, especially Black men, to wear masks and hide our vulnerabilities, there is tremendous power in embracing our true selves and sharing our stories. So, imagine my surprise that because of a chance encounter with a celebrity interview the course of my entire life has changed! I had stumbled upon an intimate conversation between hip-hop artist Jay "Young Jeezy" Jenkins and the beautiful and super talented actress Nia Long. Little did I know that this encounter would ignite a fire within me, inspiring me to embark on a profound journey of self-discovery and awareness.

As the interview unfolded, Young Jeezy's raw honesty shattered the barriers of traditional celebrity personas. With unapologetic bravery, he revealed his battle with Bell's palsy, allowing the world a glimpse into his vulnerability. In that moment, my eyes were opened to the transformative power of sharing our stories and embracing our unique struggles.

Moved by Young Jeezy's courageous revelation, I made the difficult yet necessary decision that I, too, would be unapologetically brave and tell my own story. But this is not just about me – it is about the broader connection we humans share and the catharsis that comes with expressing our innermost thoughts. Through written words, I aim to navigate my journey, shining a light on the role that faith and self-awareness play in both navigating and overcoming life's obstacles while on the path to healing. Additionally, because Young Jeezy's courage and unwavering strength inspired me, I aspire to kindle the flame of hope, faith, and awareness within the hearts and minds of others as his story did for me.

As you join me on this deeply personal expedition, it is important to recognize the significance of timing and control in sharing our narratives. The decision to peel back the layers of vulnerability in a book that friends, family, colleagues, and strangers will both explore and judge is far from easy. Yet, it is precisely this choice that empowers me to truly shape my own narrative, presenting my story in my own words while also weaving a tapestry of resilience, self-discovery, and growth!

Welcome to a chapter that promises to captivate your senses, challenge your perceptions, and leave an indelible mark on your soul. By embracing the power of awareness, we venture forth into the vast realm of human connection, reminding us that it is through sharing our authentic selves, our struggles, and our triumphs that we truly experience life!

PART 1: THE CURVEBALL

Thursday, November 9, 2023. At first glance, a day that appeared to be no different from any other day. My daily alarm disrupted a quiet morning, and as I stretched, I could already sense the familiar rhythm of life, whispering promises of a day filled with exciting plans and endless possibilities. That day was supposed to be different—I had planned a fun-filled trip to New York City that included a New York Knicks game at the historic Madison Square Garden, the Michael Jackson Play, catching up with friends and fraternity brothers, shopping, and dining at some of my favorite restaurants—all part of a grand plan for a four-day weekend, courtesy of the Veterans' Day holiday. But unbeknownst to me, fate had mapped out a different plan for me that I could not have anticipated.

Shortly after waking up, an unsettling feeling took hold—something was off. But I could not put my finger on it, and as I was not in pain, yet I was acutely aware that I did not feel like myself. In panic mode, I decided to call one of my closest friends and explain to him what was going on and that I thought I should go to seek medical attention as soon as possible. My friend agreed and urged me to go to the nearest urgent care immediately. However, there was still the matter of the trip that I had scheduled to New York City. As excited as I was for the trip, a cautious voice deep within urged me to prioritize my health and well-being above all else and I made the decision to cancel my trip. Next, I quickly jumped into action and contacted both the hotel chain and Amtrak. To my surprise Amtrak and the hotel were sympathetic and understanding and both swiftly refunded my money. It was at that moment that I realized that a twist of fate had altered the flow of my day, but little did I know, it was only the beginning!

I showered, got dressed, and took a rideshare to a local urgent care. As I approached the front door of the building, an uneasy feeling came over me. While I only had to wait twenty minutes before seeing the doctor, those twenty minutes felt like two hours, and all kinds of random thoughts were racing through my head. Specifically, I was wondering if I was having a stroke, would I look the same, would my life drastically change, and would I even walk out of the urgent care! The doctor entered the room, and we chatted about the reason for my visit and the symptoms that I was experiencing. Next, she conducted a thorough examination, revealing a diagnosis that I had never heard of and that naturally sparked a lot of questions—Bell's palsy.

Bell's palsy is a condition that causes a sudden, temporary weakness or paralysis of the muscles on one side of the face. It is thought to occur due to inflammation of the facial nerve, which controls facial muscles. The exact cause is often unclear; however some conditions associated with its development include a family history of diabetes, a tick bite, the flu, severe stress, the virus that causes chickenpox and shingles, and other respiratory viruses. My cause for experiencing Bell's palsy stemmed from a tick bite that I encountered back in August 2023. The positive news was that it is not life-threatening, and most people suffering from Bell's palsy fully recover, but the severity and duration of symptoms can vary, and the recovery is a gradual process.

The doctor prescribed me two medications, but with no guarantees attached, as there is no real treatment for Bell's palsy as it must run its course. The doctor also recommended that I see a neurologist. The following week, in the spirit of being proactive, I decided to go to the emergency room (ER) to get a second opinion and a computed tomography (CT) scan to ensure there was nothing going on with my brain or neck. The ER doctor did a series of tests and agreed with the urgent care doctor's diagnosis. He also reported that the results of the CT scan were good, and there were no signs or concerns of a stroke or brain issues. Two weeks later a neurologist confirmed that I had Bell's palsy and explained that while there is no specific treatment it would gradually get better, and possibly quicker if I did facial physical therapy.

As I left the neurologist's office, I felt encouraged, but also lost and stuck wondering, "Why was I chosen for this unexpected journey, and what lie ahead? "

PART 2: WOE IS ME

In the weeks following my visit to the neurologist, an invisible weight pressed down on me. It was like I became a hostage in my own mind, consumed by the fear of how others would perceive my potential new appearance. I was entering a dark place and the outside world felt like a gallery of judgmental eyes, each glance a potential verdict on my possible new look. I had read some literature that the doctor gave me. In that literature, I discovered a lot of possible temporary effects that Bell's palsy could have on a person.

For example, a distorted or drooping face, the inability to smile, the incapability to close the right eye, slurred speech, and the temporary inability to move one side of your face. Thinking about the possibility of all the above happening to me created high levels of anxiety and stress.

I started to withdraw to the point that plans that once brought me excitement and anticipation became casualties of my own newfound insecurities. I started avoiding meetups with friends. In fact, I mastered the art of intentional cancellations, crafting excuses like an artist paints a masterpiece because the reality was that I dreaded venturing out into a world that now seemed severely harsh and judgmental. Even when I found myself with time at my disposal, I intentionally fake busyness, dodging invitations to social gatherings to maintain solace in my own space.

In the darkness of my isolation, helplessness and powerlessness became my constant companions. There were even times I cried. Every time I looked in the mirror and tried to move the right side of my face and could not, it served as a reminder of the control that I temporarily no longer had. Eventually, as the days stretched into weeks, a cloud of sadness lingered over me, it was the equivalent of a relentless storm that showed no sign of relenting.

There was also the annoyance, frustration, anger, and anticipation of having to deal with people who make your unfortunate situation about them and people who are unintentionally insensitive. By unintentionally insensitive, I am referring to when a person says or does something that is hurtful or offensive to others without intending to do so often due to a lack of awareness or understanding and common sense. In fact, I experienced some unintentional insensitivity when I went to a dentist appointment. I informed the dental hygienist that I was suffering from Bell's palsy so that he did not think that my teeth were shifted and so that he could understand that they just appeared that way because the nerves on one side of my face were temporarily paralyzed. Naturally and understandably curious, the hygienist began to ask me a lot of irrelevant and unnecessary questions as well as make unhelpful statements. In fact, it felt like the equivalent of being cross examined by opposing counsel or being interrogated by a detective. After his sixth question, without hesitation, I cursed out the hygienist, while simultaneously explaining to him the reason for my reaction. Again, while I understood his curiosity, he did not understand that his questions were inappropriate and insensitive to me. He did not stop to think about how his questions and statements would make me feel. And lastly, his questions and comments had no bearing on the reason for my visit, which was a routine cleaning.

As I entered the fifth week of dealing with Bell's palsy, I continued to spiral, feelings of self-pity began to increase, tainting my perception of self-esteem. It also caused me to grapple with the harsh reality that my reflection slightly no longer mirrored the person I once knew. And as I sat on my couch thinking about that, the strangest thing happened. I was scrolling through YouTube, and a random video popped up of someone reciting the famous poem "Don't Quit." I felt compelled to watch it. When I was pledging Phi Beta Sigma Fraternity, Inc. in undergrad, I had to learn "Don't Quit" as part of the pledge process, and from that point on, the poem has always spoken to me, especially the following lines: "So stick to the fight when you're hardest hit, It's when things seem worst that you mustn't quit."

It was in that very moment of hearing those exact words again after so many years that I realized it was time for me to literally snap the fuck out of it and stop feeling sorry for myself. After all, I was fortunate not to have suffered any severely dramatic physical changes, and the reality was that despite my temporary condition, the world was not going to stop for me. I still had a coaching certification program to complete, a business to start up, countries to visit, a thriving career to keep excelling in, young minds to shape, people who depended on me, and most importantly, a purpose-filled life to live out to its full potential!

Hearing that poem again helped me forge a new understanding of courage. The temporary mid-grade depression that held me captive for a few weeks now served as the vessel that reshaped my perception. Bell's palsy, once a formidable foe, became a conduit for the resurgence of my faith and awareness!

PART 3: RECLAIMING ME

Since my diagnosis, my faith has been tested in ways that I never imagined! Yet, it is my faith that has become my anchor in this difficult time. It is not just my belief in a higher power but a profound trust in the process, in my journey, and in the knowledge that all my experiences, no matter how good or bad, have a purpose. Additionally, faith has taught me patience, to see beyond my immediate struggles and to understand that healing is not just about my physical recovery but the growth that comes from enduring and overcoming adversity.

Awareness has also played a pivotal role in my current journey by serving as both a guide and a protector. For me, awareness has involved being attuned to my emotional and mental states, recognizing when I am under stress or facing challenges, and understanding the impact these challenges have on my well-being. This heightened sense of self-awareness has enabled me to take timely and appropriate actions to address my needs, whether it is seeking support through therapy, adopting coping strategies such as working out and reading daily affirmations, or making other necessary changes in my life. Furthermore, as I navigate the challenges of my condition, awareness has helped me to identify my strengths and resources, leveraging them to overcome my current situation.

Part of how I have been able to maintain a fairly normal life despite suffering from Bell's palsy, is by staying focused with reading, praying, live streaming church service, life coaching sessions, working out, engaging in fun activities, and connecting with friends and family. These serve as a reminder of the positives still present in life; they are not distractions for me, but affirmations of life's joy and the importance of staying present and living fully despite my temporary challenges. Therapy has also been a tremendous help for me. In fact, my therapy sessions have become more than just appointments; they have served as opportunities for growth, and for making sense of my temporary new normal. Each session has been a step forward, a chance to reclaim a piece of myself that was momentarily lost.

My journey has not been without its struggles, but it has been filled with moments of profound growth and understanding. I have come to realize that my condition is not a barrier, but a bridge to deeper self-awareness and compassion. It has also taught me the importance of patience, of giving myself grace during times of difficulty.

In the end, my story is not just about navigating a temporary health condition; it is about transcending it! It is about tapping into the depths of faith and awareness, about finding strength in vulnerability. It is also about inspiring others to find their own path of resilience. It is a story that encourages me, and I hope others, to keep moving forward, to embrace our struggles, and to emerge stronger.

As I look towards the future, I am filled with hope and determination. Bell's palsy has been a teacher and a catalyst for change in my life. I genuinely believe I am stronger, more empathetic, and more resilient because of it! My story is one of perseverance, of finding strength in the midst of struggle. And most importantly, it is a reminder that faith and awareness are powerful allies and that when combined with a commitment to self-care, there is no challenge too great to overcome!

ABOUT THE AUTHOR

J. Artel Smith is an accomplished educator, federal employee, coach, and entrepreneur. He brings over 18 years of experience in federal funding, program/project design, employee development, strategic planning, problem solving, higher education, and organizational development.

Within that time, J. Artel worked at the U.S. Department of Justice (DOJ) as a Senior Program Manager where he designed, developed, led, and established policy for international and national criminal justice grant programs. He left DOJ in 2022 and is currently part of the senior leadership team for the largest federal grant-making agency in the federal government.

J. Artel received a Bachelor of Arts degree in Government & International Politics from George Mason University (GMU), where he is now an adjunct professor. In this role, he helps to shape the minds of young adults and prepare them for life during and after college. J. Artel has a 24-year relationship with GMU that includes being a student, faculty member, mentor, Greek, alumnus, and former VP of the Black Alumni Chapter. Additionally, he earned a Master's of Education degree.

J. Artel is also the CEO and Founder of the Institute for Transformative Thinking LLC, a full-service coaching and consulting firm. J. Artel is a proud and active member of Phi Beta Sigma Fraternity, Inc (PBS). He is also a former state officer/Area Deputy Director and staff writer for PBS.

PART IV

IDENTITY

"Identity is a prison you can never escape, but the way to redeem your past is not to run from it, but to try to understand it, and use it as a foundation to grow."

— SHAWN "JAY-Z" CARTER

16

KATHERINE N. JOHNSON, ACC, CPC, ELI-MP

BEAUTY UNVEILED

"You are your best thing."

— TONI MORRISON

THE WORK

Who are you? That's the question I was asked at the women's empowerment retreat. My usual answer wouldn't suffice. We were told that the question was not asking what we did, where we lived, or what we liked. Our answers shouldn't include any titles, roles, or responsibilities.

I felt like I was back in first grade. This time, instead of staring at the teacher, I was staring at a blank piece of paper. I remember feeling annoyed and confused. I thought my usual answer was good enough. I had said it many times with pride without thinking about it.

I half listened as the other retreat attendees shared their answers that sounded so good, deep and poetic. I didn't know what to write, so I sat quietly, staring out as my mind pondered, who is Katherine

N. Johnson. The truth was outside of my job, my titles, and my responsibilities, I didn't know.

THE AWARENESS

Imagine watching a blind person see for the very first time. Oh the awe and wonder they would experience as everything around them came into focus. With this gift of vision, they would go beyond the pictures created in their mind. They would see things as they really are and as a result, experience the world in a very new and different way.

That's what awareness has been like on my journey. It opened my eyes to what I needed to see and understand about myself so that I could grow. Awareness has gifted me with perspective, allowing me to remove a mask that kept me hidden and shed limiting beliefs, fears, and insecurities that did not serve me. With this awareness, I'm able to truly see myself to understand who I am so that I can walk in my greater purpose and vision.

My name is Katherine Nicole Johnson. Today, I proudly introduce myself with my full government name. This hasn't always been the case. Let me tell you the story of how awareness put me on to, well me. It all started with my name.

CHILDHOOD YEARS

Growing up, everyone called me Nikki. It's the nickname for my middle name, Nicole. It was the first day of first grade, and my teacher was taking attendance. She was calling Katherine, and I was just sitting there looking at her as she looked at me. I was expecting her to call Nikki. I didn't know that Katherine was my first name and everyone at school would call me Katherine. Then I heard her say Katherine Johnson, and I hesitantly raised my hand. I didn't know it then, but this was the start of different identities I would form with my name.

There are some other things that I remember vividly about this little Katherine. I loved school and I was eager to learn. I enjoyed the alphabet and number games and singing the silly nursery rhymes. Learning was fun to me. I was all about having fun. I even remember the mischievous "games" I would play with the boys in my class. I was sneaky and I never got caught so, I never got in trouble. My parents or teachers would likely never believe this because in their eyes, I was the perfect student.

That's the thing. I was smart, a great student, and I got good grades. I was striving for perfection even at this young age. My parents acknowledged and celebrated the fact that I did well in school. This was an incentive because I liked the attention and knowing they would be proud of me. Throughout my school years, teachers and classmates would call me Katherine, but at home, I was Nikki.

GROWING UP

Little Nikki was a very shy, quiet, and reserved child. She was also an introvert and very curious. Although I was quiet, I loved asking my mom questions. I would fire the questions off one after another. My mom would tell me to stop asking so many questions. I can only imagine her plight. There were four of us. She would always be doing something like cleaning, cooking, or getting ready for work. There I was asking why this and why that. On a good day when perhaps she wasn't tired or overly consumed with the responsibilities of being a mostly single parent, she would oblige me. On other days, she would say, "Didn't I tell you to stop asking so many questions." To which I would pout and go away to my room.

In my room, my imagination would run free. Asking 101 questions in my mind and making up my own stories. This is why I loved to read and write. I found all the answers I sought while reading books. I was fascinated with people, places, and culture. I wanted to know what it was like for other people growing up in different parts of the world. I wanted to understand other cultures and what made people who they were. When I was 15, I became obsessed with reading romance novels. I loved the story of how two people would meet, fall madly in love, and then live happily ever after. Sometimes I would skip to the end of the book just to make sure it had a happy ending. I was a romantic and obsessed with these often fairy-tale stories of romanticism.

Little Nikki was content and happy to be in her room reading her books. I was in my room so much that I would get in trouble for being in my room. My mom would tell me to come out of my room and come be with the family or go outside and play.

At 17 years old, I joined the U.S. NAVY. This decision was a surprise to everyone, especially my best friend. Months earlier I told her that she shouldn't join the military. When I first visited the military recruiting office with a friend, I also told the recruiter that I wasn't interested in joining. Although, something about the military did pique my interest. I had even imagined myself wearing a uniform.

Weeks later, a military recruiter showed up at my school. He took me out to lunch and explained what the military had to offer. I particularly liked the opportunity to work in my chosen career field of Information Technology, receiving money for college, and the opportunity to travel the world. I definitely had some fears, but I was more determined than afraid.

My mom asked if I was sure I was making the right decision. She had to sign papers because I was only 17 years old. My high school counselor asked the same questions. She was concerned that my demeanor and personality wouldn't be a good fit for the military. I can't explain how but I knew I was making the right decision.

MILITARY LIFE

In the military, we go by last names. Johnson was determined to do well and be successful. She joined forces with little Nikki, and together these two were on a mission to advance. Johnson excelled because, like little Nikki, she wanted the rewards that came from being good and following all the rules. She stayed out of trouble and tried to be the perfect sailor.

The military provided structure and a system that if you stayed within its confines, you could do well. This came at the cost of your identity and who you were as an individual. There was no room for individuality. Your opinions weren't important. No one cared about your feelings. You conform, blend into the system, and don't ask questions. This left me very disconnected from my feelings.

At an age when I should have been figuring out who I was as a person, I was being molded into who I needed to be. I had someone telling me what to wear, what to do, and where to be at all times. At the time I was focused on doing well. I didn't want to mess up or worse, disappoint anyone. I didn't realize the impact and how the military was shaping my very being. While Johnson was serious, focused, and determined, the curious, expressive and fun nature of Katherine was buried. It would be years before I made this connection.

During my military years, there were many times when I felt alone and lost. I felt like I was drifting aimlessly. Why am I here? What is my life supposed to mean? I wrestled with these questions in my quiet moments. However, my commitment to excelling in the military left little time to dwell on these thoughts. I chose to leave them where they were, buried deep inside.

Outside of work, Nikki was still her quiet self. I smiled but didn't have a lot of words for people and now I had a very serious and stoic military-like demeanor. With friends, I was Nikki Johnson. With a classified job and a top-secret clearance this gave me a new level of privacy. Now I legitimately couldn't talk about what I did in the military. I relished people not knowing my full government name. This added another degree of secrecy because I wasn't sharing much about myself. Instead, I was very much closed off.

CIVILIAN LIFE

With Nikki's help, Johnson did well in the military, earning many awards and accolades. After active duty, I transitioned into civilian life and continued working in the Information Technology field. At the time, I was 21 and felt like I was grown. I was introducing myself as Nicole. For my first few jobs as a civilian, I asked everyone to call me Nicole. I felt that Nikki was a childhood nickname that I had outgrown. However, to this day my family still calls me Nikki.

The rest of my 20s were full of fun. I felt like I had some catching up to do. Those were some of the best years of my life. Although I was still working to move up in my career, having fun and being with friends was a priority. I was enrolled in college and working towards obtaining a degree but at the time, having fun was more important than school. Going out helped me reconnect with having fun. When I wasn't working, I was hanging out with my friends. This meant less time alone and feeling lonely.

As Nicole Johnson, with friends, I was still quiet, shy, and reserved. Somehow most of my friends were the opposite. They helped me learn how to socialize and open up to trying new things. My friends were the best at allowing me to be me, coming to my defense, and speaking up for me. They would say leave her alone, she's fine, she's just quiet. I was allowed to stay in this familiar and comfortable place where my voice was not present. I rarely shared my opinions or engaged deeply in conversation.

CAREER

I was in my 30s, making six figures and doing well in my career. I was "successful" by someone else's standards. I had buckled down and finished school, graduating with a Bachelor's degree at age 28 and a Master's degree at age 33. At age 34, I bought my first home by myself. I was proud of the fact that I accomplished these things on my own.

From the outside, my life looked perfect. No one would guess that anything was wrong. On the inside, I wasn't happy. I felt something was missing and there had to be more to me and my life. I was questioning my greater purpose and life meaning. Why am I here? What is my life supposed to mean? I still didn't have the answers. One thing I knew for sure was, I had no desire to continue climbing the corporate ladder, pursuing more education and gaining further qualifications. My career did not feel fulfilling.

RELATIONSHIPS

One area of my life that wasn't going well was my romantic relationships. I couldn't deny that there was something wrong. A couple of years prior, I walked away from a long-term relationship with someone I loved dearly.

After ending that relationship, I immediately jumped into another relationship. I was still questioning if I made the right decision to end my previous relationship. I knew that I didn't want to be in another relationship yet somehow there I was.

This was a pattern in my relationships. I would meet someone and things would be going great. Then somehow we're in a relationship and then things aren't going so great. The relationship would end, often with me leaving and the cycle would repeat. I was always questioning if I really wanted to be in a relationship, if I was with the right person and why I still felt alone and misunderstood.

AWAKENING

By age 35, I was questioning everything. What's wrong with me? What am I doing with my life? Why do I feel this way? Why do my relationships keep failing? To answer these questions, I had to do something I had yet to do. I needed to face the mirror and tell the truth. I could no longer pretend that my life was perfect or that I was okay. The truth was, I felt a deep sense of emptiness. I had many of the things that were supposed to bring happiness. Yet, I still felt lost about who I was and what I really wanted in my life. Finally being honest about these feelings, was the turning point. I decided that I wanted to find what was missing so I could truly be happy. This is how I found myself staring at a blank piece of paper pondering the question, who are you?

The following year, in January 2018, I decided to attend my first women's empowerment retreat. I had traveled alone to Fort Lauderdale, Florida searching for answers. Deciding to go by myself was scary and completely outside of my comfort zone. However, I felt called to this retreat. I knew it was going to be the start of something beautiful. So much so, that when we were asked to create our name tags in advance, I didn't hesitate. I gave my full name Katherine N. Johnson.

UNVEILING

Through deep reflection, introspection and coaching I began the work of unveiling. My name variations over the years helped me do a good job compartmentalizing the different parts of myself. In doing so, I took on the identity of who I needed to be and what my experiences and circumstances dictated. Claiming my full name was the first step in finding and embracing myself.

Socially, I had worn the labels of quiet, shy, and introvert like a badge of honor. While these characteristics served a purpose, they didn't have to define me. I had always felt awkward when communicating out loud. I felt like I didn't know what to say or how to say it. I didn't want to sound or look stupid. I was afraid of what people would say about me. Finding my voice and learning how to communicate confidently without fear of other people's judgements was a big part of finding me.

Years after the military, I realized that I still carried the Johnson persona, showing up in the workplace how I thought I needed to be–often without sharing opinions, expressing feelings, or bringing any real facets of myself. I'll never forget when an image therapist asked me to describe my work clothes. I had over a dozen slacks and collared shirts. Each day I would grab a pair of slacks, a shirt and rotate them from week to week.

This had been my wardrobe for many years. It mimicked my military uniform allowing me to blend in with my colleagues who were mostly men. There was no femininity, no personality, and no Katherine in my wardrobe. Blending in and conforming was familiar and comfortable. It seemed like a safe and sure way to excel until it left me completely lost to myself.

My lack of happiness in my career was less about the place I had reached in my career. It was more about the person that I was choosing to be. I was being one way with family, another way with friends and a different way with colleagues. I was wearing a protective mask and a uniform that was hiding my true self. It felt suffocating because outside of this professional and well put together persona, there were bigger parts of me left unacknowledged and unexpressed. The part of me that spoke up, shared my feelings and showed my personality. The curious, expressive and fun part of me. I had to shed the parts that were no longer aligned and hiding my authentic self to reconnect with Katherine. She was ready to be seen and heard.

My relationships were merely showing me what I needed to see about myself. I never allowed others to get to know all of me. I presented an aura of perfection. Any parts of myself that I felt weren't good or perfect were hidden. I was afraid of what others would think about me if they were privy to my innermost thoughts and feelings. Embracing myself meant learning to love and accept all of me. Even what I deemed as flaws and imperfections.

I was always seeking perfection in my partners just like I was seeking perfection in myself. As a romantic, I held idealistic beliefs of what I expected from my partner which were not rooted in reality. I hadn't learned how to communicate my wants and needs. When these unvoiced expectations were not met, I was over the person and the relationship. The more I connected with my feelings and spoke my truth, the less I felt alone and misunderstood. As I learned to love and accept myself, I became more confident in myself and my relationships improved.

Gaining awareness has taken me on a beautiful journey allowing me to reconnect with my true self. It has transformed how I'm being and how I show up in the world. I no longer hide behind my names and associated identities. I no longer hide the parts of myself that aren't perfect. I am no longer silenced by limiting beliefs, fears and insecurities. Like fog being wiped from a mirror, awareness has offered a clear view unveiling the beauty in me, Katherine Nicole Johnson.

ABOUT THE AUTHOR

Katherine N. Johnson, ACC, CPC, ELI-MP serves as a Life Coach and Technology Consultant, extending support to entrepreneurs and organizations. As an ICF Associate Certified Coach (ACC), she brings her expertise, complemented by a Bachelor's degree in Technical Management and a Master's Degree in Information Technology.

Katherine discovered at a young age that she had a natural ability with technology. When asked what she wanted to be when she grew up, her answer was always a computer specialist and journalist. At the age of 17, she left home to join the U.S. NAVY and became an Information Technology systems technician.

After over 20 years working in Information Technology, she found her calling as a coach, which answered a deeper desire to use her gifts, talents, and abilities to support others. Katherine is passionate about helping women move forward confidently to pursue their greater purpose and vision. Through her own personal growth journey, Katherine has seen firsthand the power of coaching to create awareness that leads to transformation.

Today, Katherine combines her tech savvy and coaching skills to help coaches, consultants, and service providers utilize software applications as powerful tools to grow highly efficient and profitable online businesses. She has created a fulfilling business, merging her unique gifts, talents, and abilities with her purpose of serving others.

Outside of work, Katherine enjoys reading, traveling, biking, hiking and all things Zen. She loves sweating in the sauna, relaxing in the jacuzzi, being in the ocean, getting a great massage and spending quality time with family and friends.

https://www.katherinenjohnson.com

17

ALEX DAVIS, CPA, CFP®

FROM SHADOWS TO LIGHT: THE JOURNEY OF HEALING BEYOND THE FACADE

I'm sharing my story to prove that it is possible to overcome trauma and achieve all that you desire. You, too, can rise above and live a life that reflects your true worth, both inside and out. Countless women bearing heavy burdens wake up each day and carry on, presenting a composed facade to the world while struggling within. My story stands as evidence that you can endure immense challenges and still triumph. We are many, wearing our smiles amidst unseen struggles – struggles that have broken others. I share my journey not just as my own testament but as an invitation for you to embrace and continue yours, knowing you're not alone and that your story, too, holds the power to inspire and heal.

I'm a unicorn. Not a literal unicorn or I couldn't type this chapter. I'm a unicorn in the sense that my accomplishments are statistically rare. I hold two certifications in the financial industry sector. I am both a Certified Public Accountant (CPA) and a CERTIFIED FINANCIAL PLANNER™ (CFP®) Professional. These are rare feats. A CPA focuses on mastering accounting and tax laws, crucial for managing finances accurately, while a CFP ® Professional offers guidance on long-term financial planning and investment strategies. Both are essential for financial empowerment and security, and require passing rigorous exams and many years of experience in the industry.

Let's get into these numbers.

As of 2023, I am one of 0.5% of black women who are both CPAs and CFPs.

Despite the odds stacked against me, I've achieved remarkable success. I was raised in a low-income, second-generation single-parent home in the heart of Sarasota's Newtown neighborhood. In a community where father figures were absent and mothers worked tirelessly to make ends meet, my childhood was marked by a harsh reality, witnessing scenes no child should ever see. Almost inevitably, I became a single mom as a teenager. Did you know that less than 2% of teen moms graduate college before the age of 25? I graduated with two degrees before the age of 25. Yet, amidst this environment, I defied expectations and not only graduated from college but did so with two bachelor's degrees. My journey is a testament to resilience and the power of unwavering determination. So, see what I mean about my being a unicorn.

While I've shared my accomplishments, there's a deeper aspect of my life. I've survived child molestation, date rape, teen motherhood, a forced abortion, and a secret life as a mistress for over a decade. The amount of trauma I just laid out in a sentence may have broken others, but like Maya Angelou reminds, Still I Rise. Outwardly, I may seem the epitome of resilience, having faced these adversities and emerged victorious. But this strength came from a relentless push forward, often avoiding the full confrontation with my pain. Now, even as I work towards healing, I find there are still traumas too raw to face. My journey is one of continuous healing, as I learn to navigate and process the deep emotions still hidden within me. I've mustered the courage to open up about my journey because the healing I've undergone has taught me an invaluable lesson: shame thrives in silence, and not speaking our truth only keeps us in the shadows. I firmly believe that we are connected to others in profound ways, meant to support and influence each other.

Yet, this connection is impossible if we choose to hide. The internal work I've embarked on has not only been transformative but has also revealed my true gifts. I refuse to let those gifts be stifled by silence. My story is a testament to the power of voice and healing, and a reminder that we all have the strength to emerge from the shadows.

THE BACKSTORY

My journey to motherhood began unexpectedly with my eldest daughter, yet it turned out to be a blessing in disguise, reshaping my future for the better. At 18, as a senior in high school with a 4.5 GPA, I was on the brink of becoming the smartest dropout, scarcely attending classes due to severe depression following a traumatic experience. At 16, I endured a forced abortion, a decision not my own, leaving a lasting impact and a deep sense of unworthiness.

However, when I discovered I was pregnant again at 18, I made a resolute vow to keep my baby no matter what. I took proactive steps, enrolling in Cyesis, a school for pregnant teens and teen moms, and navigating healthcare systems on my own. It wasn't until 20 weeks, with a noticeably growing belly, that I revealed my pregnancy to my family, only to be met with heart-wrenching criticism from a close relative.

This painful experience fueled a lingering drive within me, a determination to prove that my life wouldn't be ruined by this choice. It took me two decades to realize that in my quest to prove my worth, I had been living for others, losing sight of my own goals and dreams. This story, this journey, has been about reclaiming my voice and embracing my path, one where I define my worth and pursue my aspirations.

The true danger of harboring negative experiences in our subconscious is their invisible influence over our lives. Unaware of their presence, we can't begin to address them. I've always been a high achiever, yet nothing I accomplished ever felt sufficient. It was an endless pursuit of goals, but I didn't understand the deeper implications until I was compelled to confront them, once in the "real world" after graduating college.

Public accounting, my first "real job" was a battleground for me, a place where my struggles with self-worth became amplified. In a non-diverse, challenging, and high-pressure environment, I constantly felt out of place and inadequate, even though there was no concrete evidence to support these feelings. I persevered for a decade in a field that I knew, three years in, wasn't right for me. As a single mom, I matched the long hours of my colleagues, passed my CPA exam, and maintained a facade of capability, all while seeking validation and battling intense stress. By 2015, the physical toll was evident: severe weight loss, insomnia, vomiting, anxiety, and hair loss so severe it looked like I had a pet in my home.

Reaching a breaking point, I sought help. At first, I tried an anxiety medication, but I soon realized it wasn't the answer for me. It was a conversation with another partner at the firm, who mentioned her therapy sessions, that led to my lightbulb moment. Hiring my first therapist was a pivotal step. In our first meeting, I understood leaving my accounting job was crucial for my well-being. This led me to embark on a journey of healing and self-discovery while paving a path out of public accounting and toward creating my own venture.

After diligently saving $24,000, paying off $50,000 in debt, and meticulously planning the launch of my own business, I left my public accounting job to devote myself to AGA Tax and Consulting Services LLC, my very own venture. My mission was clear – to help entrepreneurs manage their finances while taking back my personal freedom and time. Known for my independence and capability, I stepped into entrepreneurship with the same self-reliance.

However, this journey unveiled a different reality. The traumas I had masked in my previous job emerged in the solitary world of entrepreneurship, proving that my old coping mechanisms were no longer effective. This realization was both challenging and enlightening, as it showed me the need to deepen the personal work

I had started in therapy. My path involved investing over $60,000 in business coaching without seeing a direct financial return, not just because of the coaching's ineffectiveness but also due to my own internal battles with self-sabotage and feelings of unworthiness that blocked the implementation and consistency needed for success. This experience highlighted the crucial role of resolving inner conflicts to truly thrive in both my business and personal life.

THE TURNING POINT

Then something profound happened. I attended my first in-person retreat in October 2022. What was so magical about that weekend retreat was that I was surrounded by other amazingly accomplished women with their traumas and all just desiring to live a life of freedom. We had some massive breakthroughs, but even more powerful than that, I connected with some amazing women. We have supported one another on our healing journeys and been able to be completely vulnerable without fear of judgment. You are reading this chapter because of one of these beautiful women and her vision. This beautiful experience unlocked the level of vulnerability that I needed to take some bold steps. For the first time, I felt safe to express myself. My takeaway is that we aren't meant to live life on our own, and it's essential to find your safe, supportive tribe. After the retreat, I knew I had to explore ending my toxic relationship I had been in for over a decade because I knew I was ready to stand in my full Queendom.

Before attending the retreat, I was deeply involved in growing my tax and consulting firm. Despite investing tens of thousands of dollars, the coaching aspect of my business remained unlaunched. I was caught in a cycle of seeking external validation, and doubting whether my ideas were good enough. I created numerous packages, only to either not launch them or inadvertently sabotage them. But there came a point when enough was enough. I had the knowledge from business coaches and understood that the strategies were effective; I just had to implement them! The real challenge was identifying what was holding me back from taking action.

The retreat was a turning point. I shifted my focus from business tactics to personal growth to evolve into the best version of myself. I engaged a new therapist to help me permanently exit an unhealthy relationship and collaborated with coaches specializing in intuition, breathwork, and money mindset. I committed myself wholeheartedly to personal development. More than that, I became part of a supportive community. No longer isolated, I was actively engaging with others who were as devoted to their journeys as I was to mine. I found a circle of women who could nourish my growth as much as I contributed to theirs, a balance of giving and receiving that was both empowering and transformative.

The outcome of this transformative journey was one breakthrough after another. Not only did my business grow more profitable while demanding less of my time, but more profoundly, I began to unlock and confront traumas I hadn't even realized existed or ones I thought I would never conquer. One of those I had to confront was the secret affair I was in for over a decade. Thirteen years ago, I met a man who seemed to embody the ten qualities I had longed for in a partner. When he walked into the bank, I was convinced he was the one. Yet, a year and a half into our relationship, I discovered he was involved with someone else. Despite this, our relationship continued, off and on, for 12 years, even after we had a child together. It took all those years to finally recognize my worth and understand that I deserved so much more. The shame of being in that relationship had kept me in hiding, but through this journey of self-discovery, I started to emerge from the shadows, embracing my worth and stepping into a new light of self-awareness and empowerment. My business skyrocketed after this feat. I went on to have my highest-grossing year in my business, lose 40 lbs, and deliver programs and events that had been in my heart for years. It's been a journey, but one that was so rewarding and ever-evolving.

THE EPIPHANY

Sitting on my therapist's couch recently, I experienced a life-altering epiphany that reshaped my approach to business and personal life.

She posed a simple yet profound question: "What story did you create about your dad not being in your life?" Tears welled up in my eyes; my voice trembled as I struggled to speak. The words finally came: "I believed I wasn't good enough. Not good enough for him to stay, to search for me, or to even check-in." It dawned on me that my overachieving wasn't solely about personal ambition – it was a quest for validation, a desperate plea to feel loved, to feel worthy.

This realization was eye-opening. I understood why I clung to public accounting for so long, why I stayed with a man who couldn't fully commit to me, why I accepted clients who weren't right and undercharged—all because I didn't feel worthy. But the true beauty of this revelation lies in its empowerment. With this newfound awareness, I now possess the power to make different choices to redefine my path not by the absence of my father, but by my own intrinsic worth and capabilities.

The truth hit hard when I ventured into my own business: I was high-functioning and successful, but it wasn't sustainable. Without a company to blame for bad days or unmet goals, the responsibility fell squarely on me. I faced a critical decision: continue ignoring the deeper issues or dive into them with curiosity and courage. My therapist shared a powerful analogy: life is like a journey down a path, and our struggles are like rocks we encounter. Instead of addressing them, we often add these rocks to our backpacks, making the journey increasingly burdensome until we reach a point where we must confront these traumas to move forward. The question then becomes, how do we handle these rocks?

This revelation shed light on a broader truth: the way we handle one aspect of life often reflects how we handle others. Trauma and the subconscious patterns it creates repeat themselves until we recognize and change them or decide to cultivate new habits. For years, my response to trauma was to chase accolades and people-please, seeking validation and acceptance.

Entrepreneurship forced me to confront the root of my trauma in a way public accounting never did. In the corporate world, I had mastered the art of masking my pain. But in the world of entrepreneurship, particularly as a solopreneur, there's no "faking it till you make it." You might resonate with this. Maybe you're tirelessly working to prove your worth, or others admire your achievements while you struggle to see your value. In those quiet moments, alone with your reflection in the bathroom mirror, the reality of your journey becomes undeniable. What/who do you see? Are you seeing and acknowledging how special you are? Are you in appreciation of who you are? What other feelings or thoughts come up that know one ever knows but you?

I cannot overstate the necessity of internal work. Don't underestimate the impact of unresolved trauma; whether you're conscious of it or not, it's affecting you, often in detrimental ways. In my experience working with hundreds of women, a common barrier to achieving their goals is deeply rooted in feelings of unworthiness. This sense of not being enough manifests in various aspects of their lives: financial struggles stemming from a belief they don't deserve wealth, settling for unfulfilling or unhealthy relationships due to a lack of self-worth, and inhibited business success because of doubts about their right to succeed on their own terms. Recognizing and addressing these internal issues is crucial for genuine progress and fulfillment.

What I can confidently share is that my business is not only thriving but, more importantly, my family is flourishing due to the internal work I've undertaken. A recent incident comes to mind involving my eldest daughter, who made the decision to leave Florida State University. The devastation was palpable, and my reactions were intense – tears, screams that seemed to pierce my soul. Engaging in this internal work has allowed me to see my daughter as a complete individual with the autonomy to make decisions that are best for her. It also empowered me to utter the two most challenging words for any parent to say to their child: "I'm sorry." I apologized for my outburst and emotional reaction. The truth is, my distress wasn't primarily for her; it was about me. I had attached my sense of worthiness as a mother to external validation. The reality was that my daughter was unhappy at FSU. Once I could release my own issues, I became capable of seeing her needs and became a supportive and loving mom, which was all she truly needed.

By sharing my story and the lessons within this chapter, I aim to spark a moment of reflection and motivate you to begin your own journey of healing. I've come to understand that internal work isn't just beneficial; it's essential. Trauma left unchecked subtly influences our lives, impacting our relationships, financial stability, and overall happiness.

Consider this an invitation to examine your life. Look closely at what's lacking, what's restraining you, and imagine what could be achieved if you chose to heal and let go of these burdens. You've already accomplished so much; now think of how much more you could achieve by healing and truly liberating yourself from the silent weight of unresolved trauma. The decision is in your hands: continue on as you are or take the leap to heal, grow, and reach unprecedented heights.

ABOUT THE AUTHOR

Transforming personal trials into professional triumphs, Alex Davis, CPA, CFP®, is a beacon of financial empowerment.

As the founder of AGA Tax and Consulting Services LLC, she leverages her comprehensive expertise as a Certified Public Accountant, CERTIFIED FINANCIAL PLANNER™, and Licensed Life, Health, & Annuity Agent to offer entrepreneurs more than just fiscal guidance; she offers a journey to financial liberation.

Alex's path from a single mother in debt to a net worth of $300,000 exemplifies her commitment and skill in navigating the complexities of wealth creation. Her firm is more than a consulting service; it's a transformative experience dedicated to changing the way entrepreneurs interact with money.

http://www.agataxservices.com/

18

DYANA LANGLEY-ROBINSON

ALL THE SHADES OF GRAY

Careful now - it ain't *that* kind of book, but my story IS about lots of gray. Way more than 50, so let's start with what makes someone like me "all the shades of gray." We live in an age of categorization, and as an Operations Leader who focuses on people leadership more than anything else, I am the first to admit my love of organizing chaos to create calm. Think of the seemingly endless number of boxes we check to describe ourselves and put people in different categories. Depending on what form I am completing, I may identify myself as a Jewish woman of color with an MBA originally from Colorado or currently a VP at a Seattle Tech company. On other forms, I may be asked about my paternal roots, which can be traced back to the enslaved who were purchased in Brazil and sold in the American South, or about my maternal side which includes European Jewish and Italian heritage as well as that of British settlers in Newfoundland dating back to descendants of the Mayflower.

Perhaps this crossover of different worlds is how I became equal parts 90's R&B enthusiast, self-described oenophile and bibliophile who has taken a number of twists and turns in her career that may be seen as less predictable. An unusual recipe made from equal parts determination and a refusal to allow others to define what I can and cannot do - which is all great, but let's be real, it isn't all Instagram hype videos. It is a constant work in progress to determine what success looks like in my own gray while also accepting that success has to be a fluid state to avoid getting stuck in only what you "think" you can be.

FROM THE BEGINNING ... SO MUCH GRAY

While certainly not unique to me, many of us look to our parents as a guide to how we live our lives or, in some cases, how we choose *not* to live our lives. Understanding the moments of awareness that changed or altered the direction of my journey would begin with acknowledging how they began. My parents separated when I was two years old. There is this seemingly idyllic photo of me sitting on a window sill of our front window, staring out at a beautifully serene snow-covered Colorado day. The photo always reminds me that it was taken about the time my parents were separating and that my life, as I had known it, was about to drastically change with a shared custody arrangement. I learned early on to adapt to two very different spaces. My parents were the example of how opposites attract - from their skin tones to their religious beliefs ... damn even the cars they drove - everything was opposite. However, one common thread between both households was being surrounded by an eclectic collection of books, and it should come as no surprise that I remain book obsessed and find it impossible to leave any bookshelf empty.

Living between two different lifestyles, I found a pendulum swing of predictable measures. Mom had a presence when she walked in the room without a "stealing the spotlight" kind of vibe, and I grew up thinking she had a keen sense of balance as well as the ability to look at different sides of an issue ... what I would now call being expert level at succeeding in gray spaces. I felt there was nothing worse than disappointing her, and so as long as I didn't do that, I would be fine - spoiler alert, there were plenty of times I missed the mark.

Dad, whom I devastatingly lost in 2018, was the strong, silent type that didn't need to say much to leave an impression. He could equally fill a room with joy or suck the air right out of it, just based on how he was feeling. He had his own kind of quiet confidence but a much sterner manner. Never meant to be mean, but definitely clear about what life should and shouldn't look like. For him, I would go to college, I would be successful, I would continue to raise the bar on what he and my mother had done in their lives, and everything else would just be gravy.

Having parents of different races, religious backgrounds, and lifestyle choices added another dimension that changed how I communicated. If you live in two different households, as many kids do, you learn to do your own version of "code switching" early on. Never wanting to be less of who I thought I should be for either one of them while understanding that it meant finding a comfortable middle ground may have been difficult growing up, but became secondary to breathing for me. I didn't think about what it took to be myself in both worlds ... I just did it. It was a lesson that has served me well in my adult life because more than anything, it taught me that they could both be right. There is no one way to get to any destination and learning this when I was a kid has been a constant reminder that there can be many roads to "right", many shades of gray.

My parents' shared vision for my future was one that never wavered. The ultimate trifecta of finding what I love to do, becoming good at it and then finding a way to be paid enough to ensure my independence was instilled in me at an early age. There was never any pressure or assumption that I would have children of my own, only the assurance that doing so while working toward my goals did not make them mutually exclusive—which could feel like its own shade of gray over the years.

REALITY CAN BE GRAY AS HELL

My own resistance to fitting into a particular mold dates as far back as grade school when my first-grade teacher told me I couldn't possibly play the role of Goldilocks in a school play. My teacher's inability to envision a young brown skinned girl as Goldilocks elicited such a dramatic reaction from me that my parents were told to look for a different school. Well, it may have also been my *reaction*. Let's be clear that when the young blonde girl who didn't know a single word of the play was picked over me—who had memorized every word complete with emphatic dramatic stylings—my need to fight this seemingly obvious injustice was one that felt completely black and white to me. As I asked question after question of this teacher, she never wavered that this other girl was the better Goldilocks. When I finally couldn't take hearing this anymore, I *may* have thrown my chair at the teacher and ended up being expelled. How many kids are expelled from the first grade? There have been many times I stood up for myself and not necessarily with the best response, but my parents always heard me out and had my back.

This first dose of stereotypical bias resulted in my parents enrolling me in an amazing satellite school in downtown Denver that opened an entire new world of different cultures, music, and alternative approaches to education. My first-grade teacher's blatantly narrow-minded views activated my parent's determination to make sure my educational experience would not be limited by the misguided perceptions of others. Emerging triumphantly from this seemingly gray moment left a lasting impression.

Unfortunately, when I reached high school age, I had to transfer back to the "burbs" public school system. Back to being one of the only two Black students to graduate was an adjustment, but by this time, I had learned to channel much of my frustration and feelings of isolation into my writing. Ditching classes turned into ditching full days and hanging out with my best friend. One day, I came home from "school" to find my mother calmly sitting at the dining room table. After much creative storytelling, aka bullshit on my part,

I had no choice but to admit that I had been ditching class most days to which she replied:

> *"Dyana, this is completely up to you. If you don't want to go back to school, I will support your decision but you would need to work more hours and be financially independent. That car you want? Here are a few ads for what one costs. That apartment you have been dreaming of? Here are a few ads with rental costs. I am sure that even though you have missed a significant amount of math classes you can still quickly determine how many hours you would need to work to pay for that lifestyle."*

I didn't need to do any complicated math to know my hourly salary wasn't going to fund my dreams. What stayed with me more than anything was my mother calmly getting up and leaving me to think about what had happened without ever raising her voice. She was going to let me figure this out for myself, and my options were clear. Freedom to drop out of school but give up the things I wanted or go back to school and get my shit together so that I could have a chance at the kind of life I imagined.

I went to school the next day, graduated on time, and went on to attend university. My mother's reaction to giving me the tools and space I needed to make and "own" my decision greatly influenced how I would later approach being a leader. I learned that although awareness can be found through meaningful contemplation, it can also come in the form of the proverbial kick in the ass.

My first job was making pizzas when I was thirteen, and I never stopped. Working my way through college, it was important to me to do as much on my own as possible. I worked my way up in retail sales positions and thought it would last for years, but then 9/11 happened, and the world changed. Then another student recommended a total industry shift and one that in no way was I "qualified" to do. Call it kismet or sheer dumb luck, but I interviewed with a manager who believed individuals could be more than their cookie-cutter resume might indicate and his decision to hire me set me on a totally different path. I had literally fallen into the world of sales and management, initially in retail cosmetics, then this massive change to wireless telecommunications, and on to cable and currently technology. But I have never forgotten that initial opportunity to prove myself in a new and unexpected space. I learned that there was still enough of that same space left for me to adjust my earlier dreams without abandoning them entirely and began to find success in places I hadn't even considered. As my career progressed and my ability to provide that same opportunity to others increased, it remained at the core of my leadership style.

In my current work world, I'm usually not the smartest person in the room. In fact, I prefer being in spaces with people who challenge my thinking in ways that make me a better person. Maybe that is why I found a niche in being a people leader very early on. I have been drawn to the prospect of creating a balance between leading a group while also being strong enough to own its failures if we tried something that perhaps didn't initially work but then were able to pivot and feed off of collectively amazing minds working together to do what others considered impossible. When you can function and thrive within the gray, you are less constrained by the limits of only staying within the boundaries of what you think is expected of you. You can begin to develop a sense of self-empowerment and the confidence to explore alternative approaches.

THE DESTINATION MAY ALSO BE GRAY(ER) THAN EXPECTED

Living in the gray in a variety of spaces has worked in my favor but it is sometimes difficult to focus on my own preferences, goals or achievements without feeling selfish or ungrateful. It is easier for me to focus on others, and once I found that I was adept at finding superpowers in others where most may have overlooked, it became MY superpower. "Want to take your team from good to great? That's what I do." I am typically not the technical expert but what I do best is to lead a team of people who have hit walls or couldn't move forward. While I am able to acknowledge that ability in myself, I have also used it to create a protective wall to avoid putting my own personal and professional goals front and center. Fear of achieving them is absolutely at the center of this for me but what usually worked to help me achieve those personal and professional goals was many times to my own personal detriment.

My dad would always caution me about getting too attached to my work and that I would get nothing in return. One of his favorite quotes was, "Work harder than the next person, always - but why are you so attached? It isn't personal. It's business. But if you insist on being so devoted to your job, they better start calling you President or CEO." My favorite retort was, "Don't put all that on me—let's go for VP and see how it goes."

These past few years, my focus has been on how to manage being the kind of mother, wife, daughter, and friend that I had always wanted to be while also being determined to see IF this goal of becoming a VP was possible. That challenge became a silent way to acknowledge myself as the walking legacy of two people who had worked their asses off in ways that made it possible for me to even imagine being at such a professional level. I wanted my kids to look at me with even a percentage of the pride I felt for my parents, and I started to believe my dad's teasing wasn't just a passing joke but a reality within my reach.

Second-guessing myself hung over me like ominous clouds before the storm. I did my job and met expectations but the threatening clouds still seemed to follow me everywhere. My antidote was to redirect that energy and focus on others. I put myself in very uncomfortable situations and took on assignments that "old Dyana" would never have sought by challenging and pushing me into spaces where I had to be more vocal, technical, and vulnerable.

When my promotion finally became a reality, it was a celebrated milestone in my career, but I quickly realized that the "high" of becoming a VP could be fleeting. There had to be more to this than achieving the title alone, and what the hell do I do for a second act? Never doubting my mother's pride in this accomplishment, I felt the void of my father's absence and the loss of not being able to share this achievement with him. That loss changed the way I absorbed the moment. Not only did he miss meeting and holding his grandchildren, he didn't get to see that title next to my name. Perhaps my second act could be to maximize whatever influence came with it by having a more positive impact on the people around me.

That could be my second act and perhaps be more gratifying than the title itself or as I asked myself on a regular basis ... What was it all for?

THE "MAMA" TITLE IS THE BRIGHTEST SHADE OF GRAY

Anyone who has become a parent while balancing career goals is aware of the need to be completely nonlinear, illogical, and insanely flexible just to get through each day. Parenting is nothing but gray. In 2019, while still trying to manage being a wife, a daughter, a friend, a corporate leader, and a handful of other deeply important titles/categorizations, I also became a mother in the middle of a world pandemic. You want to talk about gray? Being a parent in today's world requires being adept at successfully managing spaces that are wholly unpredictable. My son, Avi was born in 2019 and my daughter, Liana was born in 2021. They are both what we call "Covid Kids" as they were born in some of the strangest times we may ever see in our lifetimes. My expectations about being a "working mom" were instantly shattered when Avi was less than six months old and the world literally shut down. And because the universe can at times have the strangest sense of timing, Liana was born right as the "Delta Variant" was all the news and although we had started to come out of our shell a bit, we were back to being a family of hermits.

In the midst of managing this new space of parenting during a pandemic, I somehow still had this drive to accomplish more. Now these two little humans were looking at me and my husband Jeff the way I watched my parents. What would I want them to take away from observing the lessons learned from my invariably gray choices?

The amount of pressure to be successful AND be the kind of mother I could be proud of is a shade of gray for which I was unprepared. Seeing myself through the eyes of my 4-year-old asking, "Mama, why are you always working and cleaning?" has a way of stopping me cold, leaving me to ask myself if I have my priorities straight. I still struggle to find the elusive balance that people write and talk about, but I won't give up trying. It may be years from now before I know if I made the right choices in order to navigate through all the emerging challenges of gray awaiting my kids' future and prepare them to take on the world. However, I will always remain mindful of how to leave space for them to not feel like a failure if they flip a chair (for the right reason of course) or come dangerously close to being kicked out of high school or always opt to take the less traveled roads in their lives.

GRAY IS NEVER BORING

Thinking of my ancestors on both sides who developed different survival skills and persevered in the most difficult of circumstances, I have come to value the strength and power of being able to live outside of the boxes we check and the categories we are put in and sometimes just live and thrive in these shades of gray. It is this same principle that has afforded me the space to take on roles that frankly I could have only ever dreamed about because not only can I thrive in the gray, I also find that others who don't fit in the "just right" category are prime candidates for roles and experiences that they otherwise might have missed. Being in a position to provide opportunities for success in unexpected roles and watching people flourish in ways no one had envisioned will remain a guiding force within my second act. Placing value on less traditional backgrounds and skill sets and providing the space to explore the less predictable are at the core of my approach to leadership.

There was never any guarantee that I would become a parent, so finding my way through yet another convoluted gray space will be my never-ending challenge. Anyone who meets me can usually guess that my favorite colors are black and white. Only now am I starting to have a deep appreciation for what happens when they are beautifully combined to make the most amazing shades of gray. All the shades of gray. **And gray is never boring.**

ABOUT THE AUTHOR

Dyana is a seasoned professional with over two decades of leadership experience. She currently serves as the Vice President, Global Sales Operations Excellence at F5, Inc. Her career journey reflects her commitment to individual and collective excellence, talent development, and creating diverse and inclusive work environments while fostering cross-functional collaboration on a global scale.

Committed to diversity, equity, and inclusion, Dyana serves as the Executive Sponsor for F5 Appreciates Blackness (FAB). Her intense passion for affinity groups such as FAB and F5 Connects Women has driven her to dedicate her time and efforts to multiple organizations specializing in creating equity inside and outside the workplace. Dyana holds an MBA with a specialization in Marketing from Regis University and a Bachelor's degree in Mass Communications from the University of Colorado at Denver.

Dyana and her husband, Jeff, moved to Seattle from Denver in 2015 and are still exploring like tourists with their shared love of wine and travel. These days, their explorations include family adventures with their two amazing children, Liana and Avi, while still trying to make time for the pursuit of quirky coffee shops, bookstores, and wineries to make the most of those beautifully cloudy Seattle winters.

A voracious reader, Dyana's obsession with books has resulted in the creation of an eclectic personal library limited only by the number of bookshelves she can add. Exploring and creating memories with her family and friends are her favorite ways to unwind.

PART V

MINDFULNESS & REFLECTION

"For what it's worth, it's never too late to be whoever you want to be. I hope you live a life you're proud of, and if you find you're not, I hope you have the strength to start over."

— F. SCOTT FITZGERALD

19

JANAE D. JOHNSON, M.A.

POWER IN THE PAUSE

In all things, I first give thanks to God!
I feel profound gratitude to the ancestors who paved the way and enduring love to my family for being a lighthouse.

Imagine for a moment, a buzzing world of numerous calendars, emails upon emails, multiple events every weekend for months on out… and that's just the personal stuff! We won't even begin to touch the overflow of my work schedule. Does this seem familiar? Well, hello dear friend! My name is Janae, and I am a recovering busy bee.

If you haven't heard this term, no worries, you are in the right place. For my friends who took a deep sigh or felt the mirror being held up during the visualization, don't worry, we are in this together, believe me! As you engage with this chapter, the term "busy bee," as defined by Merriam-Webster's online dictionary is "one who is very busy and active," will be used. When I consider this phrase, the life of bees, and their colony structure, the symbolism is not lost. Within a colony, there are three main types of honey bees: worker, drone, and the queen. Each bee has a specific role in the ecosystem. However, worker bees comprise the largest segment of the colony and perform the most labor to support the functions and environment of the hive.

Similar to the ever-busy bee, I used to buzz from one task to another with few moments of pause and rest between. This state of being was largely informed through external nurturing and internalized pressure to accomplish as much as possible. The need to "always be doing" was familiar and at times affirming, because it reinforced what I thought was necessary to leave a positive impression, constant production and engagement. However, this is a false truth. Before we buzz through this chapter, please keep in mind, I am recovering, heavy on the ING, from being a busy bee. Meaning, the process – or journey as I've called it – of moving away from needing to fill every day with an obligation is still very much alive and active. It is my hope that my story speaks to every reader who may identify as a busy bee, know a busy bee, is a recovered busy bee, or want to peek into the experience of a recovering busy bee. It is an honor to share my reflections and lessons of this journey in the coming pages. That said …how did we get here?

ORIGIN STORY

As a millennial raised by boomer parents, who are also quite active and accomplished, the spirit of activity and success in all endeavors was cultivated early on. Personally, I believe this was transmitted in the womb, but that is a conversation for another day. To hear my aunts tell the story, growing up, my mom had us (my sister and I) in EVERYTHING! Quite honestly, this statement is far from opinion, but factual. Even in secondary school, my friends would call me a "busy bee." As far back as I can remember, every day of the week was fully booked with an activity or commitment beyond school. Forever in an organization, serving in some capacity, or working, the concept of a free day was foreign. I'll spare you prattling on the laundry list of activities, but let's just say that maximizing and balancing a schedule was honed well before adulthood through lived experience.

This high level of commitment established an elevated baseline for what I deemed a "full plate" of commitments and responsibilities. In many ways, this abnormal baseline has aided in balancing seemingly competing priorities. What others - *honestly, most in my life* - see as too much, I have historically not held the same impression. To me, I am simply doing what I am used to; say it with me - maximizing and balancing! A dear friend of mine often jokes that most people have 24 hours in a day, but I somehow have 25. While it would be amazing to have the power to manipulate time, this is not the superpower I possess or want. *I want to teleport! The ability to think of the beach and be there at any given moment has me hooked like a bee to nectar. You'll see why later in the chapter. Okay, okay, let's refocus.* However, the sentiment is not lost on me. Extracting every drop out of the day is not truly sustainable (just keep reading), and there will ultimately be moments of awareness that disrupt the practice.

The first experience that altered my internal view of time occurred very early in life due to a near-death encounter. Growing up, my sister and I would spend every summer with our Aunt and Uncle in Franklin, Virginia. My aunt is a (now) retired career high school physical education teacher, so she always had summers off. Mind you, my father also had summers off as a teacher, but I believe the parentals wanted us out of the house... that aside, summers were the BEST! During this time, I often slept at the foot of the bed. One particular night, I simply could not get comfortable in this position. Tossing and turning, I grew exasperated and eventually changed orientation to lay like most do, with my head at the top of the bed. Imagine my shock when I woke up the next morning to see the ceiling fan at the foot of the bed, where my head would have been! Looking back and knowing what I know now from a spiritual perspective, that restlessness was my guardian angel protecting me. All the same, I was SHOOK and vividly remember thinking, "Wow, I could have died." My life nearly snuffed out just as it was starting to get good—*yes, I was an extremely self-reflective and highly aware nine-year-old.*

This and many other instances left an undeniable imprint, an understanding that time is both precious and limited, which has influenced every decision. While very early, from the moment of "the fan incident" forward, I've operated with a mindset of "if I want to, I will" and "leave a positive mark." Couple this mindset with the high expectations of my community, and a mini (albeit exhausted) busy bee was created. I could and would do everything out of a trauma response because I was afraid of not experiencing or doing for lack of time. Having zero desire to leave this side of heaven, not having accomplished much, I took everything in. Over time, the internalized pressure of doing it all has relaxed *some*, and the process of reframing my perception of time continues. Life and faith have shown that what is intended for me will be... in due time.

PIVOTAL MOMENT

While on this journey to do it all, I have acquired a beautiful tapestry of skills and interests. The achieving learner in me loves developing and mastering new concepts. Having always served in some capacity, from the hospitality committee at church to various boards, I genuinely enjoy helping others. As a result, understanding people has evolved into a refined skill and propelled me into various leadership roles. My greatest accomplishments, professionally and personally, have occurred in the wings as I've supported people in my sphere of influence to excel. The joy and fulfillment I receive from helping someone identify their objectives, set milestones, and reach (and at times surpass) their goals is unmatched. Deep reflection, dialogue, and research have revealed I am an empathetic servant leader.

Empathetic Leadership

Focuses on identifying with others and **understanding** their point of view.

Want to understand **why** people are the way they are, and this desire helps them become **great** leaders who can **connect** with many types of people and **adapt** their style depending on who they are interacting with.

Empathetic leaders take a **genuine** interest in the people around them – what makes them **tick**, what inspires them, and the way they **feel**.

Servant Leadership

Seeks to achieve a **vision** by providing strong support to others.

Prioritize serving the **greater good**. Leaders with this style **serve** their team and organization first. They don't prioritize their own objectives.

Encourages people to **learn** and **grow** while bringing their **unique** expertise and vision to the table.

Nevertheless, while basking in the light of these moments, there are also shadows. Similar to the worker bees, as they buzz around to collect and deposit nectar into the comb to create honey, it requires a lot of effort and energy. In my case, I kept trying to deposit nectar but wasn't reserving any for my own energy stores, *sigh*. I had to realize these deposits were too draining, unsustainable, and contrary to my values around reciprocity.

On this healing journey, what has become evident is that during high times of effort- i.e., serving in multiple leadership roles, starting an entrepreneurial endeavor, working 40+ hours in my full-time, being a present daughter, sister, friend, sometime lover, etc. — if I am not replenishing my energy source, the results are less than favorable.

In my pursuit of being all that I could be to everyone, I had inadvertently neglected the most treasured resource – ME!

I could hear the words of my mother echoing in my mind (as they often do since she is my truth teller and my father is my nurturer), "Janae, young people die every day, and at this rate, you may be one of them." I needed a break bad, and even considered taking short-term disability for a much-needed mental and physical break. Then my back screamed, "NO MORE" and my world came to a halt as I quite literally broke.

I am a believer and feel God really showed off when he created the human body. Think about it: we have a brain that sends signals to every system in our body that tells each part what to do, how to do it, and when to do it. So, when something is misfiring, and things are happening that shouldn't, it is a clear indicator that something is wrong. Well, for me, that something was a massive herniated disk and degenerative disk disease (DDD) in my spine. Since a softball injury, I've always dealt with nagging lower back pain. However, the herniated disk elevated this discomfort to an entirely new level, literally crushing the nerves in my spinal cord and causing severe pain and numbness in my right leg. This went on for nine months! Do you know how difficult it is to drive/walk/stand when your leg is both tingling 24/7 and numb!? My goodness, what a time.

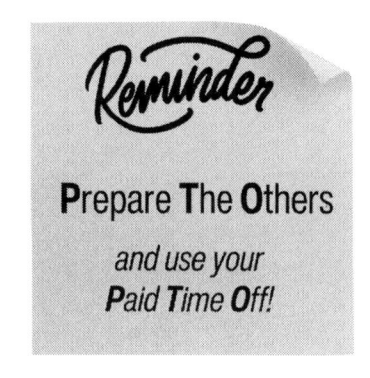

> **Reminder**
> **Prepare The Others** *and use your Paid Time Off!*

Looking back, those "deposits" in everything else came at the expense of my quiet suffering. Before we go too far, please rest assured I was actively working with medical professionals to uncover what was wrong; HOWEVER, I should have sat my hinny down. ***Y'all see this missed pause opportunity... okay, cool just making sure.*** I was so "committed" and concerned about having enough time to plan and prepare other people that when the time came to schedule surgery, because that was the only option at this point, I actually entertained the idea of delaying it just to "get through" all that was in the queue. Thanks to my wonderfully forceful sister, I QUICKLY moved away from that thought and did what needed to be done. In just three weeks, I was undergoing major spine surgery that would ultimately render me dependent on others for six full weeks. Praise the Lord for amazing family and friends who were able to stand in the gap! For anyone reading this who has lived with chronic pain and received relief, you know this, but my GOD, I didn't realize how much pain I was in until I wasn't. Even now, tears well up because it was really, really bad y'all. It is disheartening that it reached that point, but ultimately, it was God forcing me into the pause that was so desperately needed.

WHAT DOES "POWER IN THE PAUSE" MEAN?

While recovering from surgery, all I could do was focus on healing and restoration. I simply did not have the capacity or desire to feed into anything, or anyone, that was not aiding in this journey. This forced pause created space for A LOT of reflection, and some initial truths were revealed. One, I am no longer the same person; physically, mentally, and emotionally. For all that was temporarily suspended in terms of independence, I re-activated dependence, which was truly humbling as a very independent person. This time confirmed the importance of being surrounded by a supportive, capable community. Two, I LOVE not being bound by calendars and having to perform a balancing act everyday! Last, and most importantly, moving in silence is golden. There were a lot of people who had no idea what was going on with me, or that I even had surgery – some of them are finding out as they read this. By not announcing and sharing this time with so many people, I prioritized my peace, comfort, and protected the pause space that had been created.

My mother always says, "You only have one body, and if you don't take care of it now, you won't have a body to take care of." Admittedly, this may seem rather morbid; *she's a little dark*, yet she has a valid point. While some of us may believe in reincarnation, even that means coming back in a *different* form. Thus, while assigned this current vessel, my chief responsibility is to care for that body and prayerfully thrive by adopting restorative practices. The key word in restorative is REST, but too often I would press beyond what should be a pause or stopping point. Think back to the last time you felt you needed a break and didn't take one. How did you feel? How did it serve you? As a part of reclaiming my power in the pause, I applied four principles: stop, rest, breathe, and just be.

∾

Stop. Check-in with yourself and be aware of what's going on internally. After checking in, listen to the message and take action, EARLY! If you don't the universe has a knack of forcing our hand. During this season, a lot of opportunities/roles I really wanted did not go my way. At the time, I had very mixed feelings of loss and relief. Loss, for not obtaining what I really wanted and relief, because in the darkest depths of my soul I knew I should not have pursued the opportunity. As a high-achieving person unaccustomed to losing, this was a tough pill to swallow. I felt as though the universe was saying I was inadequate/undesired, when in actuality the denial was preparing space for what was to come. Thank God for His divine wisdom and grace to protect us from ourselves (*hallelujah*)!

∾

Rest. In the midst of the busyness and pain, I stopped having as much fun, doing activities I enjoyed, and resting as needed. Honestly, that last part still evades me at times. I'm getting there. Slow and steady for sustained change is the plan to which I've subscribed. For me to be the most effective and present person, power absolutely lies in the pause. The pause creates the necessary space to not completely toss ~~everyone~~, I mean everything aside. In all seriousness, taking a restorative break helps ease feelings of frustration, burnout, and apathy. These are my big three and if any of them begin to creep into the margins of my being, it is time to break away. **What are your signs to know a pause is needed?**

The Nap Bishop and author of *Rest is Resistance*, Tricia Hersey, says rest is a "lifelong, consistent, and meticulous love practice," and I could not agree more. In this powerful book, Hersey also outlines some ways to prepare our bodies for the rest, some of us, are not accustomed to taking:

"How to Prepare Your Body for Rest

1. You can not wait for the perfect space or opportunity to rest. Rest now!
2. We must believe we are worthy of rest.
3. Our bodies are a site of liberation; wherever our bodies are, we can embody rest.
4. Productivity should not look like exhaustion.
5. Deprogramming our minds and hearts from our toxic brainwashing around naps and rest will increase our ability to craft a rest practice.
6. Grind culture is violence. Resist participating in it but remain flexible. Give yourself grace."

∼

Breathe. Restoration looks and feels different for everyone, but for me, that means disconnecting and tapping into another dimension of my being. The alter ego of my busy bee is the beach bunny. My favorite way to disconnect is to travel, especially to a beach to live my best beach bunny life of sip, dip, sunbathe/nap, and repeat. If a beach getaway is not in the cards, the next best thing is solitude, specifically becoming a resident potato of couchville (aka: the couch). In either scenario, I am not on email, responding to outreach, scrolling, or anything that activates those overworked executive functioning skills. The only things I'm focused on are breathing, eating, and relaxing. These quiet, uninterrupted times of rest are the nectar I need to refill my energy stores so that I can show up for myself (full stop) and then the people I support. In this space, I'm able to fully release the breath that is often trapped in my body. Blowing out the stale air and breathing in cleansing, calming air. People will be just fine, the work will still be there, and no opportunity that is for me will pass me.

Just Be. Constantly working and not getting the rest I need simply is not worth it. The lesson in all of this is to listen to your body and the cues it gives. We only have one, and doing what we can now to be kind, loving, caring, intentional, and purposeful with daily movement, good nutrition, and restorative practices is key. Our divinely created, complex systems are not machines that are optimized by periodic maintenance. This living, breathing vessel requires a daily routine that honors the divinity within. That's my aspiration. In reality, while striving to do things daily that nourish me, I fall short. On those days, I do what I can and pray for the opportunity to try again the next day. The grace and accountability I extend to others, I also need to extend to myself. My existence is divine and necessary.

REVELATIONS

The power of my pause was transformative because in this stillness, the fog finally began to lift. Now, some of this was absolutely aided by the physical deliverance from pain, and, some of this clarity came from not being overly stimulated by everything else. After applying my four pause principles: stop, rest, breathe, and just be, I finally listened, dove beneath the initial truths, and wrestled with what was made evident.

One, when I stop, the world keeps on moving. Before y'all come for my head and think I have an overly inflated sense of self, please allow me to elaborate. For me, in my little corner of this world, there are a lot of connections and responsibilities that used to feel like I couldn't stop because then things would falter. A good portion of this belief was informed by prior experience; however, this time, that was not *completely* the case. This realization was profound because it was reassurance that when I need to put something down, my village will indeed pick it up and carry it out.

Two, as an empathetic servant leader, balance between supporting others and attending to my needs has become a non-negotiable. In order to be attentive, effective, and engaged, my cup must first be filled. Beyond taking time for myself, creating and maintaining healthy boundaries with people and commitments has been *quite* the undertaking. In all honesty, establishing, reinforcing, and communicating the boundaries that are set is *challenging*! This has by far been the hardest thing to do because of the expectations and assumptions others have placed on me. In this process, we are all unlearning and learning together. As my understanding and needs are revealed, how I am showing up in spaces and with people has begun to shift. In some cases, this hurts deeply because I genuinely want to contribute and be there for others. However, the soothing balm to this hurt is contained in the last revelation.

Three, there are many ways to still be involved and supportive without over-extending. One of my favorites is to provide an alternative that does not require my involvement. As mentioned in the beginning, with heavy emphasis on the *ING* in recovering, this is a maturing practice. Assisting others has been my default for decades. Saying no or redirecting is a shift for sure. However, I'm constantly reminded that for every no I give to someone it is a yes to me, and that is okay. More than okay, without a shadow of a doubt, it is *necessary* in order to honor what is gained in the pause.

There is great power in clarity! Now that I've had a good taste of how sweet it is to live a simpler, more defined life, I love it. Better yet, it is GLO-RI-OUS here, and awareness has indeed put me on to reinvent this bee's role. As our time together comes to a pause, I leave you with seven questions to consider as you begin or continue your own journey:

1. What challenges or pain points are you hiding from yourself?
2. How might becoming aware of them support your pause journey?

3. If you had to imagine a life full of pauses, what would that look, sound, and feel like?
4. What is stopping you from making that your reality?
5. What is one step you can take towards creating that reality?
6. Who might you invite to support you?
7. **Are you ready to reclaim your power?**

ABOUT THE AUTHOR

Janae D. Johnson, M.A., is a proud two-time alumna of George Mason University; having obtained a B.S. in Psychology and M.A.I.S. in Higher Education; and a University of South Florida alum with a certificate in Diversity, Equity, and Inclusion in the Workplace.

Since 2011, Janae has worked at Mason in varying capacities and is currently the Associate Director of Student Employment and Enrichment within the Office of University Branding. In 2020, she founded JanaeDanielle Consulting & Design, LLC to help clients identify and achieve their desired creative and event outcomes.

Within the community, she is a student organization advisor, current board member of the Black Alumni Collective, and friend of the board for George Mason University's College of Humanities and Social Sciences; Past President of the GMU Black Alumni Chapter, proud member of Delta Sigma Theta Sorority, Inc., and Alfred Street Baptist Church. Most notably, in 2022, Janae was honored as a Northern Virginia 40 Under 40 by The Leadership Center and Leadership Fairfax and a College of Humanities and Social Sciences Community and Catalyst Award recipient.

Originally from Petersburg, Virginia, Janae loves spending time with family and friends, reading, and traveling any place warm. She lives by her family motto: "If I can help someone along the way, then my living will not be in vain."

20

HADY MÉNDEZ

THAT TIME I UGLY CRIED

I will never forget the day I found out about the distinct challenges Women of Color (WOC) face at work. It was a profound moment of realization for me as I learned about the reasons why we struggle so much to climb the career ladder and why we're so rarely seen in top leadership positions.

It was the Summer of 2020. I worked at a small tech company, and prompted by the company's Black Employee Resource Group (ERG), we decided to host a Juneteenth day of learning for the entire company. We were assigned to different break-out groups for the day, and I was in the breakout room with the company's CEO.

I no longer remember the speaker's exact words but I do know that what I heard them say changed my life.

What I learned that day:

- WOC need to work twice as hard as our peers to make only a fraction of what they make.[1]
- We are subject to unfair promotion practices because of the perception that WOC are "not ready" to advance to the same level as our peers.[2]

- Our attempts to solicit useful feedback often result in comments about our personalities rather than the actionable insights we seek.[3,4]

I sobbed on the call. Ugly cried. In front of the CEO. Those tears were for me and all of the opportunities, financial rewards, and promotions that I missed out on. And for the millions of WOC whose work experiences are defined by how people see us and not by the contributions we actually make.

I felt grief and extreme sadness. I felt the pain of generations upon generations of injustice. I felt sorrow for WOC everywhere who questioned their abilities and sense of self. I felt deep sadness for young Hady whose dreams and aspirations were shattered by the broken system. I felt it all and I let it out. I knew my career journey up to that point was not everything I had hoped for and I always believed I was to blame.

All of a sudden, it made sense. My lack of promotions and raises didn't always reflect my abilities or potential. I was harmed by a broken system that was not designed for me to succeed. Even though I frequently outperformed my peers, I was led to believe that I was not worthy of rising through the ranks in the same ways they did.

Transparently, I don't really believe excellence was expected of me: a Latina working in tech and financial services.

HIJA DE BROOKLYN AND PUERTO RICO

I once referred to myself as *"Hija de Brooklyn and Puerto Rico,"* and I would say that probably describes me best. I identify as a Latina and Woman of Color. I'm the youngest of four sisters and grew up with parents who did not have college degrees or professional jobs, making me a first generation college graduate. I obtained a degree in Computer Information Systems and a minor in Religious Studies. Transparently, I've always been drawn to practical endeavors but I also give myself permission to explore things that pique my curiosity. I won medals for my major and minor areas of study, was next-in-line to the valedictorian, and graduated Summa Cum Laude. My first job out of school was at a prestigious IT consulting firm, where I worked for three years. I worked for two major financial services firms where I obtained a Certified Mortgage Banker (CMB) designation and my Series 7 License. After twenty years in corporate, I left my job to become an international volunteer. I worked with incarcerated and formerly incarcerated women in Bolivia for two years. I then went on to work at an elementary school in the South Bronx as their Community School Director. I love helping people. I currently serve on the board of two nonprofits and volunteer as a mentor, coach, and advisor to countless future leaders.

My friends describe me as feisty, hard-working, and badass. They're not wrong.

CALLADITA TE VES MÁS ~~BONITA~~ FEITA

There's a saying in Spanish: "Calladita te ves más bonita." Loosely translated it means "You are more pretty when you're quiet." I know. CRINGE.

This saying is quite common in Latinx families, and many of us are taught to adopt this mindset at a very young age. Don't talk back to your teachers, don't fight with your classmates, and always listen to authority figures.

I was one of those people who drank the Kool-Aid.

Because of this damaging belief, I never learned the skills needed to advocate for myself. I allowed others to get away with vague comments or feedback. I allowed others to dismiss my contributions or sometimes even take credit for my work. I remember joining a business development team and having more success in my first year than my two more established counterparts. I never got recognized for my achievements. I'll never know for certain the reasons why I didn't receive the accolades I deserved, but I will always be a little mad with myself for not doing more to demand it. Managers and leaders gave me less than I deserved and I settled for it.

Looking back, I can honestly say I was too *intimidated* to demand what I had worked hard for and earned. I was too *afraid* of being punished for challenging my manager. I was too *naive* to realize that if I didn't advocate for myself, I would never get what I wanted or deserved.

Sometimes it felt like the folks around me preferred it that way. The more fearful I was, the easier it was for them to overlook me without any consequences.

EMBRACING NEW MINDSETS

I had to unlearn this way of thinking and accept that remaining *calladita* simply did not serve me.

Here is a collection of other mindsets I've learned to embrace over the years:

- I own my narrative
- I share what I want and hope for
- I can ask for help in achieving my goals
- I advocate for myself and others
- I teach others how to advocate for themselves through my speaking engagements and digital content
- I am vocal about pay transparency, pay equity, self-advocacy, and self-promotion because these things matter
- I am outspoken and disruptive while still being a positive, contributing member of the teams I belong to

LETTING GO OF WHAT DIDN'T SERVE ME

I've had a long career by any standard. Over three decades of navigating professional spaces in various capacities. I've worked as a consultant, an engineer, a project manager, a strategic program manager, a product manager, a business development manager, a relationship manager, an international volunteer, a community school director, a customer success manager, a head of equality, and a business owner. I've been a team member, a people leader, and a department head. My proudest moments are the times when I've made someone else's life easier or better because of my work. I value authenticity, transparency, equity and inclusion. I've always viewed myself as ambitious, consistently striving to move forward in my professional journey.

When I think back to the times I didn't get promoted when I hoped I would, the number one reason it didn't happen was because I didn't believe I deserved it. I had to let go of this belief.

Here are some other mindsets I've had to leave behind:

1. **People will advocate for you without your specific help and guidance.** Let's pretend that folks want to help you, that they see potential in you and want to use their power and influence to help you and your career. I've learned that folks need to know how they can help you, and only you can tell them what you need. Are you looking to get promoted? Easy. Ask them to advocate for you at the table where that decision is being made. Maybe you are looking to pivot into a new role or team; let folks know how they can support you in that endeavor. Perhaps you are hoping to work with a big client or get assigned to that juicy new project. Whatever you need/want, make it known. Let the right people (starting with your manager) know what you are hoping for and remind them of it often. When something works out, make sure you are reporting back and allowing others to share in your success. In the end, you reap what you sow, so make sure you are planting seeds everywhere!
2. **Hard work and keeping your head down is a recipe for success.** I truly believe that we adopt limiting beliefs that need to be unlearned and replaced with empowering, limitless mindsets. In my case I was definitely

taught to "work hard and keep my head down". I was led to believe that I did not have to advocate for my work, that I did not have to build relationships to advance, and that I could simply rest on my laurels to get ahead. These proved to be some of the worst things I could believe in. As a WOC, it's easy to get lost in the sauce if we are not deliberately and intentionally advocating for ourselves at every turn. Pay attention and use your words to get what you want.

3. **I can succeed without the sponsorship and support of others.** I've learned the hard way that folks are busy trying to advance their own careers. It's extremely hard to get someone with the right level of power and influence to care about you without understanding what's in it for them. I try to build genuine relationships with people at all levels and from all backgrounds. But let's be honest, sometimes it's challenging to demonstrate to others how helping you will benefit them. And yet, consistent and sustained promotions and recognition won't come without their support. Moral of the story: you MUST figure out a way to get other people excited about you and invested in seeing you succeed. When asking for support or sponsorship, I like to appeal to the desire in others to amplify underrepresented voices. There most definitely are would-be sponsors out there looking for an opportunity to demonstrate their allyship. It's our job to find them. And remember, when we make our sponsors look good, everyone wins.

4. **I don't have to prove myself.** As a WOC, this is all too real. You will be proving yourself over and over again. The best thing you can do is lean into it. Have your elevator pitch ready to go and share it often. When I was a Customer Success Manager meeting customers for the first time, I would initially introduce myself by sharing my name and letting my customers know I would be their primary point of contact. That was pretty much it. I

noticed that all of my peers were sharing where they went to school, if they had an MBA, what top-tier firms they previously worked for, even sometimes name-dropping (I know such and such senior leaders at your firm). WOW! That was eye-opening for me. I quickly learned that I had to have my story in order and be ready to share it, especially when people were meeting me for the first time. Introductory calls are not the time to be humble or shy.

5. **I don't need to develop a personal brand since I am already gainfully employed.** Wrong. You heard it here. Absolutely everyone needs to have and be building a personal brand at all times. Why? Well, for starters, you need a personal brand to get promoted within your own firm. People need to know who you are, what you bring to the table, and what makes you stand out. Those are facts. In addition, if you were ever to be let go or decide to move on to another company or role, you will use your personal brand to help you get to the next step. You should not wait until you need your personal brand to build one. That's too late. You should be building one at all times.

PRO TIP: I like to keep a "brag sheet" to track all of my contributions and successes. I add items to the brag sheet as they happen so that I don't forget any of my achievements. This is an easy way to keep track of your accomplishments and share them with others. You know when your manager asks you to share your accomplishments for the past year? This is when the brag sheet will come in handy the most. You can literally cut and paste your achievements straight from your doc.

A good brag sheet should have the following details:

- What you achieved
- The date/timeframe
- The impact of your achievement on your project/team/organization

A great brag sheet will even include testimonials from people on the receiving end of your exceptional work.

I've used a brag sheet to get promoted, to pivot to a new role, to get prospects to hire me, to build a brand on LinkedIn, to put together a Speaker Sheet for my business services, and more. Think about how easy it will be to self-promote once you have your brag sheet in place!

Remember this: if you want to be celebrated and recognized, you MUST remind people on a regular basis of all the amazing things you've accomplished and the impact those things have had on others.

THE TAKEAWAY

If I could give my younger self any advice, it would be to be brave even when conversations feel scary, ask questions when situations don't make sense, and develop sponsors from the very people who don't always show their support.

Don't be afraid to reject false narratives that simply aren't true. When someone calls you "disruptive" (as one previous manager described me), ask them to provide you with examples. When my former manager explained why he felt I was disruptive, I actually viewed it as something positive. If advocating for myself and my teammates is disruptive, then yes, Mr. Manager, I am disruptive (and proud of it)!

Here are a few more tips to fuel your journey:

1. **Take inventory of yourself.** You know yourself best. I recommend you become intimately aware of your strengths and build on them. Begin this process by simply making a list of your superpowers. Ask your friends and family to help you identify what might be missing from that list. And avoid doing this: for so many years, I focused on my growth areas. Be aware of them, but don't focus on them. Dig into

what you're good at, brings you joy, and gives you life. Build that solid foundation. That is where you will have the most success.
2. **Shine your light**. I shudder when I think of all the times I shrunk myself to let others shine. If your light makes others uncomfortable, that's on them. Dim your light for no one. Let them deal with the discomfort. Focus on shining brightly and lighting the way for yourself and for others.
3. **Don't allow doubt or fears to linger for too long.** Doubt and fear will come. You will have to deal with obstacles and uncertainties on your journey. Accept these feelings. Let them come through you, but always come back to your core values and fundamental truths. Stay grounded in your abilities and in the possibilities those abilities offer you.
4. **Live your life humbly and authentically.** Be humble and know that nothing in life will allow you to sleep better than living your life in an authentic way. I rest easy because I am committed to being good at what I do, shining my light into the world, and advocating for myself and others. What you see is what you get with me.
5. **Find your community and your people.** It makes such a difference when you have a community of people who love and celebrate you and see you for who you really are. We all make mistakes but we are not our mistakes. We are not the things we get wrong. Learn to surround yourself with positive people who will reflect who you are (to you) especially when you need it the most. When times are hard and you're feeling alone, lean on your community and your people.
6. **Keep your receipts handy.** I'm trying to end this chapter on a positive note but I am keenly aware of our reality as WOC. And so, with that reality in mind, I encourage you to keep the receipts for all the things you have accomplished (i.e., your brag sheet) and always be ready to share your accomplishments and achievements.

Do not wait to be invited to share because that invitation may not come. Don't let the request for receipts rattle you. Just be prepared and stay ready.

Today I walk through the world with so much more awareness and appreciation for the lessons I've learned on my journey. Professionally, I now get to speak to thousands of people across a wide array of companies and industries. I share what I've learned about how folks can avoid the challenges I experienced by shedding beliefs that don't serve them and by adopting a mindset that allows them to truly shine. I will forever be grateful to the people who didn't believe in me because they made me stronger. Remember the lie is that you're not worthy. The truth is that you deserve it all. Use your challenges as stepping stones and always bet on yourself!

ABOUT THE AUTHOR

Hady Méndez is a Latina speaker and Employee Resource Group (ERG) coach based in NYC that works with ERGs looking to take their efforts to the next level. She is the founder and CEO of Boldly Speaking LLC, a company that is transforming the professional experiences of women and people of color by empowering underrepresented employees with the skills to self-advocate, self-promote, and capitalize on leadership roles.

With a diverse career spanning over 25 years, Hady has served as Head of Equality for a major technology firm, held multiple customer-facing roles in high tech and financial services, served as a leader across various ERGs, volunteered as an international champion for incarcerated and formerly incarcerated women, and served as Community School Director at an elementary school in the South Bronx.

Hady's academic credentials include a B.S. in Computer Information Systems from Manhattan College, and graduate certificates in eBusiness and eCommerce from NYU and NJIT. Hady serves as a member of the NY Advisory Board at Room to Grow, a nonprofit organization that works with low-income families, as well as on the Board of Pan Peru USA and the Advisory Board for the National ERG Leadership Conference.

In her free time, Hady is an amateur street art photographer and an avid podcast listener.

www.boldlyspeakingllc.com

21

SYLVEA HOLLIS, PHD

LESSONS IN LISTENING FROM MY FIRST MARATHON

On February 13, 2022, I ran my first marathon. It was the Mercedes Marathon's 20th Anniversary race in my hometown of Birmingham, Alabama. The race was an incredible physical and psychological challenge. I started running during the pandemic, but my mental training started decades prior. I would be lying if I said it was the hardest thing I ever faced. Throughout many of my adversities, my Uncle Stacey often reminds me: "Life is a marathon, not a sprint." I remember him saying this well before I started running, but it took on a whole new meaning when I began.

Running a marathon was easier than coming out to my biological and church family. It was easier than living in a conservative hotbed while an undergraduate. Running a marathon was easier than moving to a tiny village in Upstate New York to pursue a master's in museum studies. It was easier than being a Black queer southerner in Iowa while studying African American History during my PhD program. I met each obstacle by breaking it down. Training. Often failing. Fixing. In essence, I learned how to learn what was required. I learned (subconsciously) this approach to adversity from years of watching one of the most resilient people I ever met—my father.

In the late 1990s, my dad's doctor recommended that he have a lung transplant and referred him to a lung specialist. His primary doctor posited that Dad could possibly live an additional five years if he had the surgery. For obvious reasons, we did not ask what the prognosis would be without surgery. At the time, I was in my junior year of high school. The news was terrifying. Dad had lived with sarcoidosis (a chronic autoimmune disease in a similar family of lupus) since the early 1970s before I was born. He also had it before he met my mother. Yet, this health event in 1998 was the first time I understood the gravity of the diagnosis.

My dad opted not to undergo the lung transplant surgery. It proved to be the right decision. He has lived over forty years with sarcoidosis (including over twenty years longer than the initial doctor said was possible). By medical accounts, he is a miracle. But what I see is the power of faith, focus, and family. This chapter examines all three, and what growing up alongside my father's sarcoidosis taught me about the power of awareness.

I learned about awareness from watching my parents work hard to manage my dad's sarcoidosis. My mother and father handled the range of symptoms of sarcoidosis by being proactive. They (back in a time before Google) researched the diseases' impact on the body and ideal treatments, and took seriously the environmental factors that could enhance Dad's quality of life.

There's a painful truth about what Dad's diagnosis meant for his medical care. Black bodies who are forced to interact with medical professionals—some who struggle to see the individuals behind the charts—often experience the additional stress that comes with hoping to be treated humanely. My family has too many stories of visiting doctors for help regarding Dad's condition and realizing they did not fully understand his condition or sarcoidosis in general. I learned to bear witness to my parent's form of caretaking. My mother and father made phone calls, subscribed to various free health newsletters, and chatted with other patients in different waiting rooms. By the late 1980s, they had collected a top-notch medical team—finding specialists in otolaryngology, pulmonology, dermatology, optometry, and more. Over time, they eventually needed an endocrinologist because the most effective treatment—a cocktail of medication including the steroid prednisone—had a side effect–diabetes. I am an only child, but sarcoidosis occupied space in my youth like a petulant sibling. Back then, I only noticed that the disease was why we couldn't play basketball for very long, why we couldn't go on long walks through the neighborhood, or why he would sometimes say, "We can't do that today," after he'd promised to do something just a few days prior. If sarcoidosis was like having another sibling for me—it was probably like living with a sister-wife for my mother. But that is a realization that has only come to me as an adult. In real-time, my childhood seemed quite normal even though my father's doctor visits were ubiquitous. The child-in-me looked forward to the visits. My parents brought plenty of snacks. Smiling nurses gifted me with candy. While we waited for the doctor, Dad would spin me around on the doctor's stool. The youth in me giggled secretly in the office (and later loudly on the car ride home) when Dad lied to his doctor. My father even made me his accomplice at times. "Yes, I'm walking. On good days, I jog too! Sylvea rides her bike while I follow." For years, I giggled about the little lies Dad had told. But the older I got, the more I thought about the why behind the lies. He was doing the best he could, and when asked to do more—he did not know how to say no…not until he absolutely had to.

Dad ran a marathon every workday. Not literally—but figuratively. The day-to-day work Dad did in his job as a principal was more than enough to keep him active. He arrived at school so early that he regularly beat the janitor. Eventually, they fell into a gentlemen's pact. Dad, rather than the janitor, would unlock the school—including classrooms. In return, the janitor knew he was expected to go far and beyond during regular school hours. Teachers at the first school where he was principal nicknamed dad "The Phantom" because he quietly walked the halls, and they never knew when he was near or far. Dad walked around the cafeteria during breakfast and lunch and used the time to chat with students. He made sure that every child received a meal—regardless of meal card status. I know this because I'd overhear him telling mom about having to step in after seeing a cafeteria worker pull children from the line. He eventually started giving the woman who ran the cafeteria a blank signed check—to cover the monthly costs of students whose meal plans ran out. By the time Dad came home and played with me, he *had* done enough.

I was an only child, but I was not my father's only child. In his role as principal, he became a father figure to hundreds of children. My best example is the memory of a kindergartener who sneaked onto a city bus and rode it to the opposite side of the city. The little boy wandered into a McDonald's and asked for a "Happy Meal." Upon being asked where his parents were or where he lived, the only useful thing the child said was his name and, "I go to McCaw Elementary, and my principal is Mr. Hollis." In the early days of cell phones, my dad received a phone call from the Roebuck Police Department. At the time, he was on his way to pick me up from school. In a surreal twist of fate, my mom's car had broken down that day, so he had just picked her up. I remember delighting in the extra time to hang with friends. Dad usually was the first or second car in the pickup line. But, after the second-to-the-last student was picked up, I noticed the sun's light had shifted and purples, pinks, and yellows came into view at Red Mountain's edge. I grew a tinge worried and began to think about contingency plans. The school doors were locked. Just as I built up the courage to knock on the door of a house across the street and ask to use their phone, I heard a car barreling up the large cobblestone driveway of the school. It was my father and mother. After picking up mom, dad had driven to the other side of town to attend to his student and ensure that their parent picked them up before the police moved to next steps.

Sarcoidosis exacted severe fatigue and discomfort on Dad's body, but a cruel irony of the disease is that the havoc it causes internally is rarely visible externally. For example, I remember arriving at church early to help Dad decorate for an upcoming event. (He's always early by at least 45 minutes for things—sometimes more. I later understood that he did this so he would have time to rest.)

After walking me through the plans to prep the space, a church member walked in and asked Dad to go downstairs. She had brought a piece of furniture from her home and wanted Dad to bring it upstairs. If Mom were there, she would have somehow distracted the lady by either giving Dad a more serious but less physically rigorous task or convincing her they both needed something from downstairs. I froze for a second and then told the woman, "I'll do it." Just as I spun toward the door, she said something about Dad being a tall, strong man who did not need his daughter's help. She was being light and silly but also unaware. I looked in Dad's eyes, and he said, "No, Sylvea....I'll go get it. Thank you." He returned quickly, and for a second, I marveled at his pace. But, then, he stopped midway down the aisle. Buckled for air. Her smile shifted. As she rushed to relieve him, I said, "Daddy has sarcoidosis. It affects his lungs." A look of fear came into her eyes, and I saw her spiraling through what to do next. "What?!! Why didn't you tell me?!!" I knew why Dad did not tell her, but I did not know why I was silent. That day, however, became the last day I was silent about his condition.

I went from silent witness to vocal advocate. I quickly would say, "I'll do it," if someone asked him to do something physical. Rather than letting a person tell me "no," I tried to get the thing done before they noticed I had even begun. In high school, I researched sarcoidosis for one of my classes. While studying the disease for a research paper, I learned of a new explanation for Dad's ongoing skin troubles—another diagnosis: sarcoid arthritis. It explained his wide range of symptoms as well as their unpredictable nature. Dad took the paper to his dermatologist, and they used it to engineer a new treatment plan. I chose with care who I told about my father's condition. It was not a thing for everyone to know—I only told the people I hoped would carry the message one day. Sarcoidosis needed a cure. "Never heard of it...what's that?" was a common phrase most people said after I shared. "Well, have you heard of Bernie Mac? Bill Russell? They have it. It attacks your organs. People do not know why—but it is a chronic inflammatory illness. It's not curable. It's also not obvious to people when people are not well. Flare-ups can be very scary. But there can be whole months and even years when the disease is dormant. It's unpredictable." Watching my dad live with sarcoidosis has taught me to strive to live fully with him and define what living means on our own terms. We get to decide how we run this race.

My preparation for the marathon required a consistent focus on my body, mind, and spirit—in ways that I had never intentionally given. In fact, I used to think that *that much* reflection was selfish. But I now see it as selfless. I have a family history of hypertension, diabetes, and sarcoidosis. How could I not do all that's possible to try to minimize future health risks? I learned to think more holistically about challenges and focus less on things I cannot change. It has been better to find a flow from within.

I felt so exuberant in my run across the starting line of my first marathon that I quickly decided to ignore my original race strategy to "start slow n' steady and build for negative splits." Meaning, do not push too hard. Run the second half of the race quicker than the first. Let momentum build. Rather than sticking to the strategy, I leaned into something that felt more opulent and luscious—I lost myself in every mile. My playlist was too good to go slow. The surroundings filled my mind with entangled memories and histories. Sometimes, awareness looks like consciously allowing oneself to let go. Find ways to embrace life despite its challenges.

By the time I reached the city's civil rights district, I slowed briefly to take photos of the sites. Hordes of racers sped past without turning their heads. I felt a cognitive dissonance between what I had set out to do and what was happening. I wanted to talk to others about the sacred grounds in our midst. In the 1960s people faced death in those streets in hopes of making tomorrow better. We ran past the Sixteenth Street Baptist Church, the site of the 1963 church bombing. Kelly Ingram Park is across the street from the church. It is a place where the city's local movement became internationalized. Images ran through my mind of the city's school children being attacked by the Birmingham Police and the Birmingham Fire Department on the front pages of newspapers from all over the world. Within the same block, we ran past the Birmingham Civil Rights Institute—one of the first places I had ever visited in Alabama that unabashedly told the story of the movement (and a place where I once had the honor of working).

As a young person growing up in the 1980s, the state school curriculum did not include the modern civil rights movement. Our Alabama History field trip was to the First White House of the Confederacy and the Alabama State Capitol. The tour guide explained how "happy the slaves were" and that Jefferson Davis and his family took good care of them. I have often thought about that irony, and even wrote about it in an article called "The African American History Survey as an Intellectual Product." In it, I posit that the critics of today who say children are "too young" to learn about race and racism often ignore how historically embedded racialist narratives are in our foundational histories. For example, my classmates and I were not taken across the street from the state capitol to Dexter Avenue Baptist Church. We could have learned about the Montgomery Improvement Association's successful bus boycott. A network of grassroots activists organized a protest for 381 days—with a young Dr. King at the head. But my classmates and I, many of whom were also in the first generation of our family to attend desegregated schools, were taught to think of benevolent white masters and passive Black slaves. I later came to realize after living near New England, the Midwest, and the Mid-Atlantic—that the South was not the only place where primary and secondary school curricula virtually erased African American history. During my years in graduate school, I learned from classmates and undergraduates the type of histories they were taught as young people. Many of those stories were equally disturbing.

The initial 18 miles of the marathon felt like everything I had hoped. My parents ran a good bit of the race with me. I had planned to talk to them on the phone during the early miles—to stay steady and slow. But, I soon realized I could not talk much because of my faster pace. Instead, I asked them to tell me various stories about their upbringing as I ran through different parts of the city. My stamina faded in the last eight miles. By mile twenty-one, I was painfully aware of why starting slower was not just the smart thing to do but the right thing. My legs felt like they were moving through a thick substance—weighted down. My feet ached. The frigid weather and steady pounding had made them feel numb for most of the race. My quads and calves were tight. I felt like I could not run another mile. So, I walked–anxiously. The race had a "balloon lady" who walked the full marathon. She swept up stragglers, and according to lore—if she passed you—your race was over. It is hard to focus on the finish line when you keep looking at where you have been. But that is exactly what I did. I'm pretty sure I could have had a much better time if I had just focused on putting one foot in front of the other and then repeating. However sometimes we must do the wrong thing to fully understand the right thing. I finished my first marathon successfully.

My life of running has taught me to be patient with myself and extend grace. Life does not get easier, but my ability to face challenges has improved. I work hard not to leave my body—to *feel* emotions. Examine them. Listen—even list my anxieties. Look at them. Ask each one, "Is this true? Why am I concerned about this? What led me to think about 'this' while experiencing 'that'?" On November 16th of 2024, I'll run my second marathon. This time, I plan to stick with my race strategy.

ABOUT THE AUTHOR

Sylvea Hollis, PhD is an Associate Professor of African History and African American History at Montgomery College, where she also teaches courses in Women, Gender, and Sexuality Studies. After earning a History PhD from the University of Iowa, Hollis accepted an inaugural NPS Mellon Postdoctoral Fellowship in 2018. Her current research and public humanities work explores the intersections between race, gender, sexuality, archives, and memory.

22

B. MARIE ADAMS

2:00 AM WAKE UP CALL

Here in lies Beth Marie Adams, devoted mother, daughter, sister, and friend. Beth was known for her volunteerism, giving her time and money selflessly. You often heard her asking, "How can I help?". She will be truly missed. Beth leaves behind her son Brandon, age 11, and her siblings Inga and Camille (Jerome). She is also survived by a niece and two nephews, Kennedy, 12, Ethan, 7, Channing, 5, and a host of cousins, friends, and coworkers.

Yeah, 2023 could have been the end of my earthly story, but GOD and His 2:00 AM wake-up call transformed my 2023 and set me on a new path. But I'm getting ahead of myself. Let me rewind and paint you the picture that led me to have not just one but two close calls in February 2023.

In 2020, like many people, during the height of the pandemic, we moved my elderly Mother, who lived in New York at the time, closer to my siblings and our homes in Maryland. My Mother, who was a three-times-a-week dialysis patient, had suffered a fall and hip bone fracture. Her hospitalization led to a long road of recovery, full of additional hospitalization and rehabilitation.

My entire life, I've been a self-proclaimed "Giver." I was always willing to help, rarely saying no, even when I had other conflicts. With my Mother's health turn of events, to my laundry list of titles such as Mom, Sister, Daughter, Leader of an Enterprise 24/7 IT operations business unit, Entrepreneur and Startup Founder, STEM Volunteer Instructor, Farmer, a newly inducted Member of a historically Black Greek organization, Girl Trip and Class Reunion Organizer, Friend you call to bail you out or bawl your eyes out to; I then added part-time caregiver. Although my eldest sister took on the lion's share of our Mom's caretaking responsibilities, this last title was the hardest to wear in my forty-plus years. Watching the woman I thought invincible and indestructible begin to slip before my eyes was difficult, even as a person whose life is rooted in the Christian faith. As I write this, I fight back the tears. I am thankful to GOD for the days, weeks, months, and years I had with my Mother. I wouldn't trade a moment of her time here with me for anything.

On January 16, 2023, my beautiful Mother, Sarah Adams, passed away surrounded by her daughters. We buried her on January 28, 2023, surrounded by family, friends, and the community that loved her.

Almost two weeks after burying my Mother, an unwavering presence of love and comfort in my life, I found myself on the verge of joining her, my father, who had gone on to glory sixteen years prior, and the eight other family members we had laid to rest since the start of the pandemic.

From late 2019 through 2023, I conducted and organized more funerals, created more programs, and made more slideshows than I'd ever wished upon anyone. It was so bad that people told me I should start a business hosting virtual funerals. Umm, no. Heroes, mentors, "second parents," "play uncles," and friends were all among those we've said laid to rest over the years. The toll of it all culminated with the loss of my mother.

At the same time, I worked in a high-pressure position within the United States federal government. It was high pressure not because of what we do but the political climate that I had to navigate; think Game of Thrones meets Office Space. My days were full of walking a tightrope, just trying to get my job done without hurting someone's ego and avoiding picking sides between feuding parties. At night, after working remotely, I'd log off, start cooking dinner, and immediately start on my second role as a Mom to an amazing, ACTIVE son. Oh no, I didn't get one of those kids who are happy hanging out in the house. I have a kid who always wants to be outside, whether walking at the park, riding bikes, or playing sports. And speaking of sports, he plays year-round sports. No one told me that when I signed him up for football it would be four days a week from June to November. Or that basketball is three nights a week from October to March/April. I spent weekends running between sporting events, swim lessons (oh yeah, he swims too), volunteering, running my side hustles, starting a farm with my siblings (another story for another time), attending business and sorority events/meetings, and trying to make time to check in on friends who are also still reeling from grief and post-pandemic depression. Phew, is it as exhausting reading this as it was living it? Someone asked me once if I had a hobby, and I said, "Sleep. I don't get to do it as much as I like, but I'm trying to get back into it."

Following the passing of my mother, I returned to the chaos of my life, or at least I tried to, but then, on the morning of February 14, 2023, at 2:00 AM, I was attempting to turn in for my typical four-hour nightly sleep. As I began to dose off, I felt like my heart was racing extremely fast. I heard bubbles of crackling water when I attempted to take a breath. I lay there momentarily, thinking I needed to relax and calm down. But my heart rate continued to speed up like I was running on a treadmill. Breaths were becoming harder and harder to manage, and the sound of water in my ears was felt in my chest with each attempt. It was a gurgling sound. I knew something was wrong. I recalled something my Mother, a chemist by profession, always said. "If you feel like you might be having a heart attack, take an aspirin."

I reached into my nightstand, where I kept my aspirin, and took one. Being a single mother, the fear of falling or having my son find me unconscious or worse drove me into action. I called 9-1-1 emergency services. In between each labored breath, I choppily got out "My n-name (breath) i-sss Beth (breath) Adams (breath) and I'mm (breath) having a heart (breath) attack." I gave the operator my address and begged her to stay on the phone. "I can't (breath) go down (breath); it's just (breath) my son (breath) and I (breath). He can't (breath) find me (breath). He can't (breath) find me (breath)."

Do you know how people say a parent can call on this superhuman strength in high adrenaline, life-threatening, or endangering situations as a means to protect their children? I live in a three-story home, and I had to open the door for the EMTs. The EMT responders, hospital employees, and anyone who hears this story cannot believe what happened next. I tried to wake my son, but he was in a deep sleep, and I couldn't draw enough breath to yell. So, with nothing but my phone and faith in GOD, I walked/stumbled down the hall, down the first flight of stairs, taking a break on the second floor and continuing to speak choppily to the emergency operator. I held on to the railing and slid/stumbled down the last flight to the front door, unlocked it, and opened it.

It was still dark, with no sign of the sun, indicating how early it was. It was a windy morning, and as I unlocked and opened the glass screen door, a large wind blew directly in my face. And for the first time, I inhaled deeply as GOD sent the air and oxygen my lungs needed desperately. I felt a presence and calm take over me. After a few deep breaths, with the operator still in my ear, I turned back into the house to wake Brandon. I didn't want him to be awakened by the EMT workers or fire department. With my newly inflated lungs, which still had a water-bubbling sensation, I crawled back up the stairs to my second floor and paused; I crawled up to the third floor and into Brandon's room. I shook him awake and said, "Baby, (breath) wake (breath) up. Mom-(breath)-my's not okay (breath) get up (breath) love." Brandon woke dazed and rubbed his eyes, but when they finally focused and saw me, he jumped out of bed, and I directed him to get dressed.

Now… imagine being ten and waking up to your parent crawling, barely breathing, and telling you they are not okay. My son's face, filled with fear and agony, the grief of his beloved grandmother still fresh, will remain burned in my mind for a lifetime.

I had just slid, stumbled, and crawled back to the second floor when I heard the EMT knock and announce themselves. I could finally stop moving and allow the adrenaline to wane because my son wouldn't wake to find me gone.

Before we departed for the hospital, I called my sister to alert the family to what was going on. I called Brandon's best friend's mom, who is also my business partner, to grab my baby and take care of him in my absence. I spent six days in the hospital. The doctor said my cardiac event was a heart attack, which led to Pulmonary Edema. My lungs had filled with fluid, and it was like drowning on dry land. My heart was overcompensating to keep me alive. At 42, the life of the party, organic only eating, never done a drug, rare social wine drinker, and six months prior restarted working out six times a week…ME. The words like heart attack, unchecked blood pressure, and pulmonary edema were all thrown around. I had a heart attack, and doctors were discussing congestive heart failure. I could not believe it. Oh, and the aspirin, my mother's voice in my head at the height of my stress, reminding me to take it; the aspirin helped save my life.

Two weeks following my discharge, I was readmitted for five more days due to another pulmonary edema event. The second was not as life-altering as the first time because I knew the signs and heard the crackling sound of fluid when I breathed and immediately was taken to the hospital. At this point, my family had temporarily moved in to care for Brandon and me. My sorority sisters, friends, coworkers, and neighbors had flooded my house with provisions, flowers, and get-well cards. I'll never be able to express my immense gratitude to my village.

So, what in the world brought me to the near-death experience? I spent most of 2023 thinking about how in the world I ended up in that hospital room not just once but twice. I deliberated, read, and traced the roots of my deteriorating and declining health. It took a minute to narrow it down. I masked it well, even to myself.

I realized with a profound epiphany that I was a "people-pleaser," and those behaviors wreaked havoc on my life both physically and mentally. Now I know that when people think of People Pleasing, they think of someone running behind a group trying to be included, willing to do anything to be accepted. That's one spectrum of people pleasing, but how about the "Self-Sacrificing Giver" side? Most people describe me as one of those incredibly nice and helpful, always ready with a "yes" in her mouth. Going out of my way to do a favor for a friend or coworker in need. Does this sound familiar?

This realization came with the understanding that people like me are often the kindest and most helpful individuals you'll meet. We're the nurturers of the family or the "mother hens" of the friend group. The doting parent that's lost their own identity. We're the ones who never say no, always ready to lend a hand. Our lives revolve around doing things for others and trying to anticipate their needs. We're the ones who do our work and are always available to help others, plan everything, and take care of all the details. In our quest to keep everyone happy and content, we often self-sacrifice, putting others before ourselves.

I found myself constantly busy, doing things for others, taking care of all the details, and trying to anticipate everyone's needs. In my efforts to keep everyone around me happy, I often self-sacrificed, putting everyone's needs before mine.

This continuous effort to please others came at a significant cost. While helping others made me feel good temporarily, it was a never-ending cycle. There never seemed to be an endpoint where I could relax, as there was always more to do for others. I struggled to express my wants and needs, often denying any personal issues because I didn't want to burden others. Over time, I became overworked, overstressed, and overcommitted. The guilt of being unable to "do it all" weighed heavily on me. Despite the positive outcomes of helping others, my excessive people-pleasing behavior had negative consequences. I feared rejection, had lowered self-esteem, struggled with making independent decisions, and found it hard to set healthy boundaries. I neglected my health and well-being, became silently angry and resentful, overwhelmed with the need to avoid people, and diminished in my ability to enjoy life. The stress led me to a state of chronic exhaustion, affecting my mental and physical health.

The negative consequences of my people-pleasing habits were significant:

Neglecting Myself: I devoted little time to my health, always prioritizing others. This was a fundamental cause of my health decline. Because I ignored signs and dealt with fatigue, headaches, and other signs, something was wrong. Stress and grief were mounting, and I wasn't dealing with it. I've learned that balance is crucial. Taking care of myself means I can be healthier and more energetic to help others. I also prioritized who gets access to my gift of giving. I can't save the world; I have finite time and had to decommit and cut back on activities.

Passive Aggression and Resentment: I became silently angry and resentful over time, particularly when I felt unappreciated or taken advantage of. This resentment damaged my relationships with family and friends.

Reduced Enjoyment: My excessive commitments increased my stress levels, reducing my ability to enjoy life and be present in the moment.

Stress and Depression: The chronic stress from trying to please everyone was overwhelming. I had to learn to start saying no and setting aside time for myself.

Being Taken Advantage Of: People often exploited my inability to say no, which made it imperative for me to learn to set boundaries.

Throughout 2023, I cultivated fourteen strategies to help me break this toxic cycle. By embracing these strategies, I've begun to break free from my people-pleasing behaviors. It's a journey, not a destination, and every step towards asserting my needs and boundaries is a step towards a healthier, more balanced life.

1. **Delayed Response:** When asked for a favor, I started saying I would think about it, giving myself time to evaluate my ability to commit.
2. **Setting Time Limits and Boundaries:** Agreeing to help, but within specific limits, became crucial.
3. **Realizing I Have a Choice:** Understanding that saying "No" is a choice was empowering.
4. **Setting Priorities:** Knowing my priorities helped me decide what to commit to.
5. **Identifying Manipulation:** Recognizing when I was being manipulated, the play on my emotions or weaknesses, was vital to resisting undue pressure.
6. **Creating a Mantra:** I mentally prepared to say no to habitual favor-askers.
7. **Saying No With Conviction:** Learning to say "No" without over-explaining was challenging but necessary. You don't owe anyone an explanation.
8. **Using Empathic Assertion:** Acknowledging others' needs while expressing my inability to help balance understanding with assertiveness. It also lessens any guilt you might feel.
9. **Starting Small:** Setting small, manageable boundaries helped me build up to larger ones.
10. **Not Apologizing Unnecessarily:** I always did this, even when the situation had nothing to do with me. I stopped apologizing for things that weren't my fault.

11. **Facing the Fallout Without Fear:** Understanding that saying "No" wouldn't necessarily harm relationships was a breakthrough.
12. **Choosing Who to Help:** Deciding whom I want to help clarifies my priorities.
13. **Recognizing Successes:** Acknowledging my progress in setting boundaries became a source of encouragement. I journal my progress and celebrate the small victories of "No."
14. **Accepting My Limits:** Realizing that I can't always make everyone happy and it's not my responsibility to. That has been liberating. It is easy to slip back into old habits, but awareness of the slips and seeing the pattern of behavior is progress, be that it may be incremental, but it's still progress.

Now, I won't say I've mastered all these strategies. Each day, I try to find new tools to deploy. I give you my cautionary tale as an example of what years of self-neglect, wearing multiple hats, and overcommitting could do to you. I am on my road to a full, sustainable recovery. As I write this, my cardiologist has cleared me to resume exercise, travel, and live fully while maintaining a healthy heart diet with exercise and a medication regime. It took the look on Brandon's face that night to know I wanted to be here for him and his children like my mother was for me.

Don't wait for a 2:00 AM wake-up call to prioritize yourself.

ABOUT THE AUTHOR

B. Marie Adams is a multi-faceted serial entrepreneur, international bestselling author, advocate for Black women-owned businesses, and a seasoned IT professional with two decades of experience. She has spearheaded significant IT initiatives affecting millions nationwide and developed highly successful mobile apps and websites within the banking, entertainment, and educational sectors. Recognized with numerous awards, including executive recognitions and Presidential acknowledgments, B. Marie is also a key figure on software governance and standards boards.

In 2016, she founded Entreherneur, a network aimed at uniting Black female entrepreneurs, which quickly grew to over 2,500 members. Under her leadership, the network launched the Entreherneur Foundation in 2019 to support Black women-owned businesses with grants. B. Marie also established the Brown Aspiration stationery brand in 2018, celebrating Black culture and beauty, which has grown into a leading brand offering a wide range of products.

Furthermore, in 2021, B. Marie, alongside her siblings, founded Pepperidge Promise LLC, purchasing land in Maryland for a Mental Health and Wellness Retreat. Her commitment extends beyond business as she actively mentors and supports various technology and STEM-focused nonprofits, including co-founding Sapphire Rise, Incorporated in 2023, a nonprofit serving the Maryland community.

A devoted single mother, B. Marie balances her professional and entrepreneurial ventures with nurturing her son. They share a love for reading, cooking, and playing games together. She resides in Anne Arundel County, Maryland, where she continues to inspire and lead in her multiple roles.

ACKNOWLEDGMENTS
WITH LOVE, CHANTÉE L. CHRISTIAN

In bringing this book to fruition, the journey was indeed a transformative pilgrimage, living up to its title in profound and challenging ways. There were many instances when it seemed as though the universe said, "**OHHHH**…you want to be put on to awareness? Well, here you go!" I had to use so many of the tools, techniques, and resources that are shared in each of these chapters to stay the course so that we could produce this wildly amazing book that I am extremely proud of.

I wouldn't have survived this without the help and support of so many people. I won't name them all (for the sake of saving paper), but I will name a few. To our publisher, **Kayleigh O'Keefe,** of Soul Excellence Publishing, I know my ideas and thoughts were a tad Aquarian at times, and yet, you stuck in there with me. Thank you for helping make my dream come to reality. You were my sounding board and one of the reasons I didn't close up shop…*every other day for the first 3 months…lol*! I appreciate you and your gift. Thank you for saying yes to my vision and reminding me that it was given to me for a reason.

A heartfelt thank you to our incredible foreword author, **Randi B.**! Your resounding "YES" means the world to me. Not only for this book but as a Black woman, being able to see you live your life unapologetically authentic inspires me to do the same. I truly appreciate you and pray that you never stop showing up as Randi B.! To our book cover designer, **Ida Brown,** talk about pressure making diamonds! I know I pushed you to the edge, andI'm so happy you trusted the process and helped me create something that the world can now adore just as much as I do!

To all the **authors** who contributed to this exceptional collective masterpiece…you all changed the game! You all embraced the challenge of rewriting history by sharing vulnerable stories that defy conventional concepts of leadership. I had a vision of creating a book that took leadership and flipped it on its head. I asked you all to be vulnerable and share things others would have shied away from, but not you. Each and every one of you stood up to the challenge. THANK YOU for your courage, inspiration, motivation, transparency, and most importantly, vulnerability. Thank you for allowing me to help you amplify your voices so that others can benefit from the lessons you have learned.

I'd like to extend a heartfelt thank you to **myself**. Yes, I know, I'm borrowing a page from the playbook of a few celebrities. Amidst my personal storm of fears and drama, I recognized the significance of not missing this moment, which required me to cease and desist my own internal BS! For that, I give myself a **HUGE** well done. Because it required me to not only acknowledge the call that God put on my heart but to trust Him with it the same way He trusted me with it. I made the conscious choice to set aside my fears and be obedient so that we could bring you this extraordinary collection of lived experiences.

Lastly, and certainly not least, to all of our family, friends, and supporters, we thank you for your commitment to supporting us and our projects. Most of us are recovering people pleasers and truly want to make sure you had a wonderful experience as you went on this unparalleled journey of awareness with us.

FOOTNOTES

Samantha J. A. Armstrong

1. Brown, Brené. *The Gifts of Imperfection: Let Go of Who You Think You're Supposed to Be and Embrace Who You Are*. Hazelden Publishing, 2010.
2. Smith, L., Neville, H., Barlow, S. H., & Khawaja, R. "The Role of Trauma History in the Health and Wellness of Black Women and Girls." In *The Oxford Handbook of Traumatic Stress Disorders*, edited by V. M. Follette, J. I. Ruzek, & F. R. Abueg, 187-203. Oxford University Press, 2018.
3. Brown, Brené. "In You Must Go: Harnessing the Force by Owning Our Stories." Accessed May 4, 2018. https://brenebrown.com/articles/2018/05/04/in-you-must-go-harnessing-the-force-by-owning-our-stories/.

Andrew Beamon

1. The Hustle. "Why 70 Percent of Millennials Have Impostor Syndrome." Accessed on 20 January 2024, https://thehustle.co/why-70-percent-of-millennials-have-impostor-syndrome/.

Hady Méndez

1. American Progress. "Women of Color and the Wage Gap." Accessed on 14 January 2024, https://www.americanprogress.org/article/women-of-color-and-the-wage-gap/.
2. SHRM. "The Broken Rung Is Stunting Career Growth for Women of Color." Accessed on 12 January 2024, https://www.shrm.org/topics-tools/news/inclusion-equity-diversity/the-broken-rung-is-stunting-career-growth-for-women-of-color#:~:text=For%20every%20100%20-male%20employees,leaders%20are%20women%20of%20color
3. Davis, Darreonna. "Black Women Are Less Likely to Get Quality Feedback at Work That Impacts Their Earnings and Leadership Opportunities Over Time." *Forbes*, June 15, 2022. Accessed on 11 January

2024, https://www.forbes.com/sites/darreonnadavis/2022/06/15/black-women-are-less-likely-to-get-quality-feedback-at-work-that-impacts-their-earnings-and-leadership-opportunities-over-time/?sh=1249b77f7b7a.
4. HBR. "Women of Color Get Less Support at Work. Here's How Managers Can Change That." *Harvard Business Review*, March, 2019. Accessed on 15 December 2023, https://hbr.org/2019/03/women-of-color-get-less-support-at-work-heres-how-managers-can-change-that.

Nayshondra Mercer, CPC, ELI-MP

1. Brown, Brené. *The Gifts of Imperfection: 20th Anniversary Edition.* New York: Random House, 2020.
2. *Genesis 37:1-36; Genesis 39-45*

ABOUT SOUL EXCELLENCE PUBLISHING

Amplifying the Wisdom of Conscious, Courageous Leaders

Since 2020, Soul Excellence Publishing has amplified the wisdom of conscious, courageous leaders from around the globe.

Featured titles:

- *The Empath Leader: Your Ultimate Guide to Authentic Influence*
- *The Diversity in Humanity: A New Vision for Harmony in the Workplace*
- *The Great LeadHERship Awakening*
- *The X-Factor: The Spiritual Secrets Behind Successful Executives & Entrepreneurs*
- *Black Utah: Stories from a Thriving Community*
- *Significant Women: Leaders Reveal What Matters Most*
- *Leading Through the Pandemic: Unconventional Wisdom from Heartfelt Leaders*

https://soulexcellence.com/

Made in the USA
Columbia, SC
02 November 2024